Gardening with
WILD PLANTS

Gardening with
WILD PLANTS

Julian Slatcher

GUILD OF MASTER CRAFTSMAN PUBLICATIONS LTD

For Pru
My strength and inspiration

First published 2000 by
Guild of Master Craftsman Publications Ltd,
166 High Street, Lewes,
East Sussex BN7 1XU

ISBN 1 86108 165 0

Edited by Mason Editorial Services (paul.mason@appleonline.net)
Illustrator: Liz Pepperell
Designer: Jane Hawkins/Malcolm Walker
Cover design: Ian Smith
Typeface: Amerigo and Frutiger
Colour separation: Viscan Graphics P.L. (Singapore)
Printed and bound by Kyodo Printing (Singapore)
under the supervision of MRM Graphics, Winslow, Buckinghamshire, UK

10 9 8 7 6 5 4 3 2 1

Picture acknowledgements All pictures copyright Julian Slatcher except: p.50 (left, Harry
Smith Collection); p.55 (right, Pru Dunning); p.74 (left, John Slatcher) and p.142 (Pru Dunning).

Contents

INTRODUCTION

T HE WILD PLANTS of Britain equal in beauty those of any other land. Who could deny the glory of a bank of snowdrops or daffodils, or the sweet charm of the soft, yellow primrose in spring? What garden isn't richer for containing honeysuckle or bluebells? And what gardener could fail to appreciate the rich-green colour and intricate form of a fern, or the hum of bees around a foxglove?

In Britain as in nearly all other nations, the exotic has cast its influence in our gardens. Plants have been brought in from foreign climates to decorate British gardens from the earliest times. The Romans, for example, took plants with them practically wherever they went. Some of the plants brought to Britain were medicinal herbs, some culinary and still others just reminders of a distant homeland. The most noticeable of these imports today is probably that stalwart of English woodlands and parks, the sweet chestnut.

Almost all gardeners use at least some of the innumerable species and varieties that have arrived in our countries in the hands of explorers and plant hunters,

Glorious wild plants: on the left a blaze of colour in a Staffordshire meadow, above a front-garden rockery in Pembrokeshire.

or been brought to us by colonizers or conquerers, sometimes even at the expense of our native plants. Despite their great popularity in Britain, for instance, the plants of South Africa were rarely used in the gardens of that country until quite recently: many people there preferred plants that reminded them of Europe, such as roses and delphiniums, foxgloves and paeonies.

Today we are at last realising the importance of growing plants in the places where they will be happiest; of using those plants that will thrive in their conditions, rather than struggling to keep something alive which does not really belong. Using wild plants in the garden is not something to be seen as a purely altruistic act, though. Yes, it helps to preserve the species that we use, but at the same time we are using them for their own merits. They are there to be selected from in the same way as the better-known garden plants, in order to produce the garden that you want.

My purpose here is not to tell you what you should or should not grow. Garden design, like interior design, is too much of an individual thing for anyone to be able to do that. Rather, my aim it is to present more possibilities, not less; to re-introduce to the gardening public some of the overlooked gems of the British countryside. These wonderful plants must have been the starting point for Britain's worldwide fame as a nation of gardeners and they still have a valuable place in the garden. Some we already use but do not think of and value as wild plants; others are not commonly seen anymore but would add immeasurably to any garden in which they were planted.

Julian Slatcher,
March 2000

Ribbed melilot, ragwort and wild parsley combine to give a splash of sunshine, even on the dullest day

The delicate form of a lady fern seen against the background of a sun-drenched stream

Chapter One

❖

Mixed Borders

MIXED BORDERS

A MIXED BORDER can be defined as one which includes annuals, perennials and shrubs. The inclusion of those shrubs, as well as adding structure and form to the planting and maintaining at least a modicum of interest through the colder months, when the annuals and most of the perennials have died back, also means that a variety of micro-habitats is formed within the border. There will be little spaces under the edges of shrubs or behind them, as well as between them, which give plants placed there some shelter, if not shade and a drier

SPRING MIXED BORDER

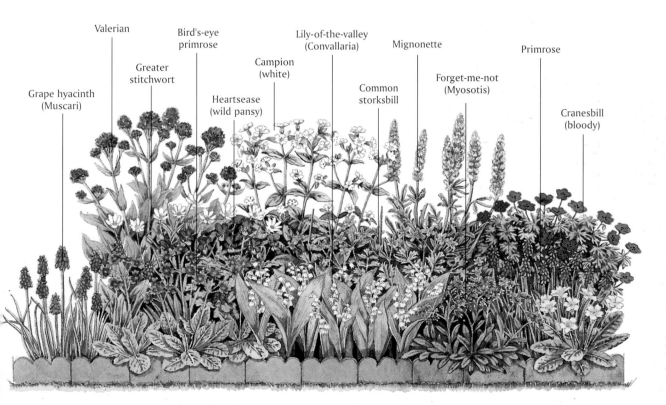

Valerian

Bird's-eye
primrose

Lily-of-the-valley
(Convallaria)

Mignonette

Primrose

Greater
stitchwort

Campion
(white)

Forget-me-not
(Myosotis)

Grape hyacinth
(Muscari)

Heartsease
(wild pansy)

Common
storksbill

Cranesbill
(bloody)

root-run than they would have otherwise. In front of the shrubs, though, is a different habitat, more like a meadow situation, where sun-lovers will thrive. Tall plants can be mixed with shorter ones here to give a variation of form and height through the seasons as well as bringing together plants from very different natural environments.

This is the place where plants which like damp soil can grow close to those which like dry; plants which like shade can grow with those that like sun, and plants which like shelter can grow with those which can tolerate an exposed site. Each protects the others and gives them the conditions which they need. viper's bugloss (*Echium vulgare*) can grow in front of columbine (*Aquilegia vulgaris*), while wild mignonette (*Reseda lutea*) stands tall behind the common mallow (*Malva sylvestris*) and lady's mantle (*Alchemilla vulgaris*) is protected by

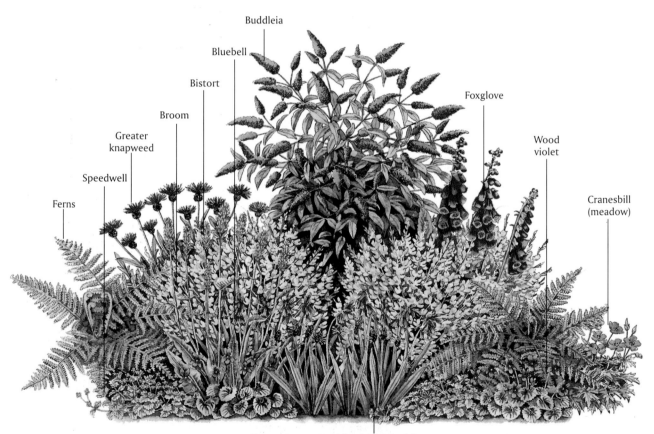

EARLY SUMMER MIXED BORDER

marjoram (*Origanum vulgare*). Here Jacob's ladder (*Polemonium caeruleum*) can stand behind the common poppy (*Papaver rhoeas*) and toadflax (*Linaria vulgaris*) can shelter self-heal (*Prunella vulgaris*) and be fronted in spring by the small grape hyacinth (*Muscari neglectum*). Colours can mix and match, with different combinations being separated by shrubs, ferns or grasses, and plants which would not grow anywhere near each other in nature can be combined effectively.

This melting pot of plants needs careful consideration before planting begins, but it is the one place where normal restrictions do not apply. Almost anything goes here, so you can really be adventurous and creative, and above all have fun while making something uniquely your own.

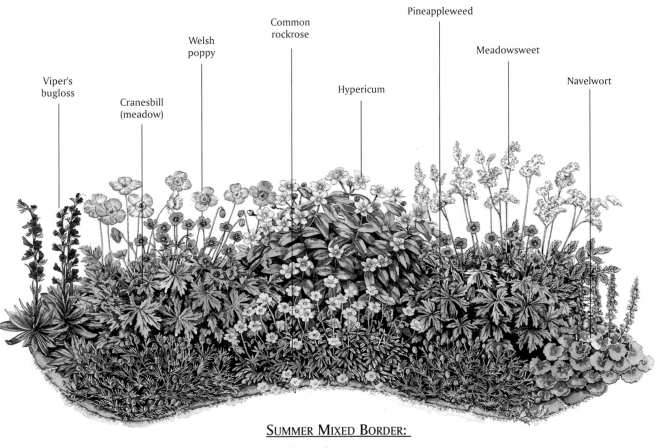

SUMMER MIXED BORDER:

JUNE–SEPTEMBER

Bistort – Common

Polygonum bistorta

Also known as knotweed and snakeweed: both of these names, as well as the Latin *bistorta*, refer to its twisted roots. There are several commercially available varieties, many of them bred for the garden from introduced species, mainly from Asia. The young leaves are edible and the long spikes of tiny flowers make a fine display in the garden from May to August. The flowers of the wild species are a soft pink in colour, born in spikes up to 7.5cm (3in) long. They are held high above the leaves on narrow stalks. The leaves are a long oval shape, indented at the base and slightly crinkled in appearance, like the docks to which they are related, though smaller, being up to 20cm (8in) long.

Height: 60cm (24in).

Habitat: Damp meadows, old scrub and deciduous woods. Can tolerate sun or semi-shade, damp or dry soils.

Garden care: Water in well when planting and until established. Cut back to ground level in late autumn, when a mulch of organic matter will be welcomed. Lift and divide clumps every two or three years to keep to required size.

Propagation: Plants and seed available from nurseries and garden centres. Existing plants can be propagated by division every two or three years.

Celandine – Lesser   *Ranunculus ficaria*

Unrelated to the greater celandine (*Chelidonium majus*), which is of the poppy family, this little member of the buttercup family grows from small tubers, which put out fibrous roots and smooth stems up to 20cm (8in) long in late winter. The leaves are on long, slender stalks and are roughly heart-shaped, with wavy edges and a shiny dark green colour. Leaves growing from the flower stem are much smaller, with shorter stalks and a more triangular shape. The flowers, borne from February through May, are bright yellow and up to 2.5cm (1in) across, with six to ten narrow petals around a boss of stamens and a green central ovary. The plants can produce long runners by which they can spread to cover a large area, so are best kept confined in containers, as you would the mints. A very attractive little double-flowered variety is available in garden centres.

Height: 15cm (6in).

Habitat: Hedge banks, woods and meadows.

Garden care: Keep watered through the growing season, which ends soon after flowering is finished in May with the plant dying back. Keep containerized in order to confine growth to where you want it. Can be allowed to dry out through the summer and brought back to life again by beginning watering in late winter.

Propagation: Plants are available from nurseries and some garden centres. Can be propagated from runners or from bulbils formed in the leaf axils.

Chives

Allium schoenoprasum

With its little balls of pink flowers carried on long, slender stalks, this bulbous perennial could be mistaken from a distance for thrift (*Armeria maritima*). Closer viewing will reveal the difference, however, for chives do not have the low mat of foliage which is a characteristic of thrift. Instead, the tubular leaves are almost as long as the flower stalks, which appear over a long period from May through July. Chives form tight tufts of rich green in the mixed border or on the rockery. They look very good edging a path, from where the leaves are easy to pick for salads or soups or to eat with cheese. There are also white-flowered and giant forms available.

Height: 25cm (10in).

Habitat: Damp meadows, river banks and path edges. Can tolerate damp or dry soils; grows best in rich soil, but flowers better in poorer ground. Needs plenty of sun.

Garden care: Remove flower stems as the flowers finish. Cut back foliage as it turns yellow with age or in late autumn.

Propagation: Plants are available from nurseries and garden centres. Clumps can be lifted and divided every two or three years in spring or autumn.

Columbine

Aquilegia vulgaris

Also known as granny's bonnet, the columbine takes its common name from the Latin for dove, describing its bird-like flowers. The native purple form is a plant of open woodland, but has been cultivated for so long that an infinite variety of shades, from white through cream and pale pink to red and purple and almost to black, can be found in gardens all across the British Isles, along with the red-and-white double form, 'Nora Barlow'. The columbines are prolific self-seeders and almost never come true to colour, so any combination of colours may be found in the garden planted with these charming perennials. The leaves are divided into rounded segments, each one usually having three well-defined lobes. They are of a soft greyish-green colour and form a bushy basal rosette in early spring, before the flower stalks rise in May. These have a few leaves, usually less divided and more elliptical in shape, and are branched. There are several to a plant, each branch being topped by one or more flowers from May to July. The seed pods which follow the flowers are narrow, upright and goblet-shaped, opening at the top when ripe and rattling in the wind.

Height: 50cm (20in).

Habitat: Open woodland, grassland, fens and wet woods, usually on lime-rich soil, though this is not essential.

Garden care: Water in well when planting, dead-head regularly to prolong flowering and cut down stems in late summer, leaving the basal rosette of leaves into the winter. In mild winters these may remain, otherwise they will die back with the first hard frosts.

Propagation: Plants and seeds are available from garden centres and nurseries. The plants rarely come true from seed, with the exception of the double 'Nora Barlow', but the mixtures of colours are very pretty and you will be hard pressed to find one that is not pleasing. Seed can be saved towards the end of the flowering season and sown in pots or trays of compost or where the plants are required in the garden.

Cranesbill – Bloody

Geranium sanguineum

One of several pink and red perennial species of hardy geranium, this upright, hairy native has deeply divided leaves and often solitary long-stemmed, cup-shaped flowers of a deep cerise or magenta colour. It begins to flower in May and, with regular dead-heading, can be persuaded to continue until well into September. The prominently displayed flowers are about 4cm (1.5in) across, with a long central spire of male and female reproductive parts which turn into the familiar crane's bill fruit. There is a very decorative cultivated form, *G.s. lancastriense*, which has light-pink flowers with deep-red veining.

Height: 30cm (12in).

Habitat: Dry grassland and scrub, woodland margins, rocky outcrops and dunes. Prefers a sunny situation.

Garden care: Water in well when planting, but watering should not be needed after that. Dead-head regularly to prolong flowering. Cut down old stems in late autumn.

Propagation: Seed and plants freely available from garden centres and nurseries. Propagate by seed or by division, digging up and splitting the clump in spring or autumn and replanting the new, smaller clumps, watering them in well.

Feverfew

Chrysanthemum parthenium

Its aromatic foliage is the main reason for growing this plant in the garden, the stems being much branched and the leaves being light and deeply divided, be they a green, silver or yellow-leaved variety. The plant makes a pleasant mound of feathery foliage, which many people keep in the border by clipping off the 2cm (0.75in) white-petalled daisy flowers, which appear from July onwards on surprisingly stiff stems. This is a smaller relative of the border pyrethrums and although it is a perennial, is often grown as an annual for edging or dot plants in formal bedding displays.

Height: 10–45cm (4–18in).

Habitat: Cornfields, roadsides and waste ground.

Garden care: For all its delicate appearance, this is a tough little plant. Any normal soil in sun or light shade will suit. Once introduced, feverfew will self-seed freely around the garden, so the chief maintenance task will be pulling out unwanted plants or digging up and repositioning them. If just the foliage is required a pair of clippers will take off the flower stems in late summer. Otherwise, the small daisy-like flowers are quite appealing and are carried in profusion.

Propagation: Seed is available from garden centres and nurseries and is best sown in early spring in trays or pots. A little light heat will help speed up germination, but is not essential. Plants can be bought later in the season from the same sources, though the green-leaved variety is usually only available from more specialist wild-flower nurseries. Semi-ripe cuttings can be taken in late summer and rooted in pots in a cool, shady place. Seed can be collected from plants, if allowed to flower, and sown in early autumn or the following spring.

Fumitory – Common

Fumaria officinalis

The weak stems of this grey-green annual will sprawl across the ground or scramble over other plants, spreading out over an area up to 60cm (24in) across with their branched, slim growths and filigree much-divided leaves. From these arise upright spikelets of usually red flowers with purple tips, though there is a white-flowered form. The flowers are tiny and tubular, about 1cm (0.5in) long, ten to fifteen of them forming a flower spike about 5cm (2in) long. A very useful and pretty plant for filling in with subtle colour among other, more vivid plants.

Height: 30cm (12in).

Habitat: Field edges, roadside verges and gardens.

Garden care: Often pulled out as a weed, this plant will probably introduce itself to you of its own free will. If it does, you are lucky. Just break off the stems when they spread too far, dead-head when the flowers fade and save a few seeds at the end of the flowering season, which lasts from April to October.

Propagation: Seed is available from specialist nurseries if the local bird population does not introduce it free of charge. Sow in pots or where it is to flower in autumn or spring.

Grape Hyacinth   *Muscari neglectum*

Bulbous plant with slightly succulent grass-like leaves, almost evergreen. A dense spike of blue flowers is produced on a stem up to about 20cm (8in) long in April or May. Each flower is small and cup-like, hanging downward. Modern garden varieties often have larger flowers than the wild plant, and are sometimes a deeper blue. A white-flowered variety is also available commercially.

Height: 22cm (9in).

Habitat: Meadows or open woodland, often on chalk soils.

Garden care: Best planted in autumn. Prefers well-drained soil and sun.

Propagation: Bulbs can be bought from the garden centre or nursery, though these are often of related species rather than this native one. A similar native species which is available commercially is the Small Grape Hyacinth (*Muscari botryoides*). This is slightly smaller and has sky-blue flowers. Clumps should be divided every three years or so.

Harebell   *Campanula rotundifolia*

Closely related to the other bellflowers, mentioned elsewhere in this chapter, the harebell is a truly lovely plant which should be included in any sunny garden. Confusingly known as the bluebell in Scotland, its 2.5cm (1in), pale-blue bell flowers are displayed from June through to September. Although the flowers are nodding, the tight buds are upright on the fine stems. The stem leaves, mainly towards the bottoms of the many stems, are long and narrow, and pale green like the stems. The basal leaves, present in early spring, before the flowering stems rise, are long-stalked little tooth-edged circles. Overall, a delicate, dainty-looking gem of a perennial.

Height: 50cm (20in).

Habitat: Meadows, dry grassland and rock or scree slopes.

Garden care: Water it in well, but it should not need watering again once established. Keep slugs at bay, if not planted in a rockery, where they are unlikely to visit anyway, and dead-head to improve flowering season.

Propagation: Plants and seed are available from specialist nurseries. Seed can be saved from existing plants and sown in pots or where it is to flower in autumn so that it germinates in spring, after the cold of winter.

Jacob's Ladder   *Polemonium caeruleum*

Though rarely found in books on wild flowers, this useful border perennial is a native of most of Europe, including the British Isles, and has been cultivated in gardens since at least Roman times. There are several forms, but generally it is an upright plant with finely divided pinnate leaves in a rich, dark-green colour and rich-blue, five-petalled flowers with golden stamens displayed prominently from their centres. It is the leaves that give the plant its name, the leaflets being narrow and rung-like, but it is the flowers for which it is grown in the garden. They begin to open in May and will continue throughout the summer. Cultivated forms include a white variant, large-leaved scrambling ones, some with blue flowers, others with pale pink, and several larger-flowered ones, though these are crosses with or bred from non-native species. There is also a very attractive variety with small variegated leaves.

Height: 60cm (24in).

Habitat: Dry grassland and hillsides. Will grow in any soil type, in sun or partial shade.

Garden care: Add compost to the soil when planting, dead-head regularly to prolong flowering; provide some support, whether by staking or by close association with other, stronger-stemmed plants; and cut down the dead stems in autumn.

Propagation: Seed and plants are freely available in garden centres and nurseries. Once established, the plants should self-seed freely, though individuals are fairly short-lived. Best propagated from seed.

Lady's Mantle
Alchemilla vulgaris

There are several closely related species of lady's mantle, many of them introduced down the centuries for garden use. All look very similar, though some are smaller or more upright than others. A very adaptable plant, it will seed itself freely around the garden once introduced and can grow almost anywhere, from wet woodland to damp meadows and rocky mountain summits. Often used as a path edger in the garden. It has light-green palmate leaves with toothed edges which are softly hairy so that they retain drops of water on their upper surface after rain. The flowers are born in soft, branching panicles which look like yellow froth above the round, lobed leaves from May to September. This hardy perennial is almost evergreen, retaining at least a few leaves through the winter.

Height: 45cm (18in).

Habitat: Widely varied, from wet land to dry and from sun to shade, though it grows best in damp shade.

Garden care: Water in well, as you would any other plant, but this one will take very little looking after from then on. Just cut away dead leaves through the year and dead-head, more to prevent excess self-seeding than to extend the flowering season.

Propagation: Most plants sold, unless you go to some of the smaller or more specialist nurseries, are of *Alchemilla mollis,* an introduced species which makes an equally good garden subject. In either case, once introduced the plant should self-seed around the garden. You can also lift and divide the plants every two or three years.

Mallow – Common
Malva sylvestris

A bright, cheery green plant, standing up to 1.2m (4ft) tall, though it is herbaceous, unlike the garden varieties that are so commonly available. (These, however, are best cut down almost to ground level in early spring, as you would roses.) The mallow is liberally covered in pink flowers, 5–7cm (2–2.75in) across, throughout the summer. It makes a bold statement if allowed room in the garden, but can take a little crowding. In these conditions some of the stems fall flat to the ground and spread out to smother the competition, while others stay upright.

Height: 1m (3ft).

Habitat: Fields and grassland.

Garden care: Although this looks like a delicate plant, in this case looks can be deceptive. Given plenty of sun, the common mallow can tolerate most soil conditions and some crowding.

Propagation: Seed is available from some nurseries and garden centres, and plants are becoming more widely available. Once you have a plant, the seeds are easy to collect, the fruit being in the form of curled 'nutlets'.

Mallow – Musk

Malva moschata

A graceful plant with deeply divided light-green leaves up to 7cm (2.75in) across. The pale-pink, near-round flowers are almost as large as the leaves, borne above the leaves in loose groups in July and August. The name derives from the smell the plant gives off when in a warm place, especially noticeable if it is used as a cut flower. A white-flowered form is available from some nurseries and seen in the wild.

There are several other mallows native to Britain, all usually found in the southern counties. Common mallow (*M. sylvestris*) is a taller plant, reaching 1m (3ft) or so. Its leaves are much less divided, almost palmate in appearance, the flowers darker, petals narrower and separated, the tips divided.

Often there is a purple marking near the base of the petals, sometimes forming a stripe down their length. The leaves are edible and can be used in salads. Large-flowered mallow (*M. alcea*) has leaves similar to those of the musk mallow, but flowers more like those of the common mallow.

Dwarf mallow (*M. neglecta*) has five-lobed, undivided leaves and pale-pink, purple-striped flowers about 2cm (0.75in) across. Its stems grow to 60cm (24in) and trail along the ground. Marsh mallow (*Althea officinalis*) is a velvety-grey plant with pink flowers up to 2.5cm (1in) across.

Height: 1m (3ft).

Habitat: With the exception of the now quite rare marsh mallow, all the mallows like dry, sunny locations such as field edges, roadsides and meadow land.

Garden care: These velvety-leaved and stemmed plants with edible nuts are adapted to heat and sun. After watering in when planting, they should easily look after themselves in most soils.

If the nuts are not required, the plant will benefit from the flowering stems being cut down after flowering. Old leaves should be left on the plant over winter to afford some protection against frost.

Propagation: Seed and plants are available from specialist nurseries and some garden centres. The nuts can be split and the seed inside them sown in gritty compost in late summer or spring.

Marjoram
Origanum vulgare

The aromatic leaves of this hairy plant are used to make a herb tea, while an oil extracted from it was once used as a painkiller, in the days before aspirin and paracetamol. Also, the pinkish-purple flowers, borne in clusters at the tops of the stems and to a lesser extent in whorls further down, were used to produce a purple dye for woollen cloth. This is not, however, the marjoram used in the kitchen: that is a Mediterranean species, *O. onites*. Marjoram is usually found growing wild in dry grassland, open woodland and sunny hedgerows, often on lime-rich soil. It blooms from June to September. There is a golden-leaved variety, Golden marjoram (*O. vulgare* 'Aureum') which flowers less prolifically and over a shorter period, from August to September, but is highly decorative simply for its leaves.

Height: 60cm (24in).

Habitat: Dry, sunny grassland and woodland edges.

Garden care: Marjoram is related to the mints, though it is less invasive, and needs similar treatment. Grows well in pots or window boxes or as a front-of-border plant. Benefits from cutting back quite hard after flowering to keep the plant fresh.

Propagation: Plants can be found in many garden centres and nurseries. Pot-grown plants can be planted out from spring through to autumn. Established plants in the garden can be lifted and divided in spring.

Masterwort
Astrantia major

A member of the carrot family, though you would not think so from the exotic-looking flower heads, this stately plant has long been popular in gardens. There is a large range of cultivars available, some with variegated leaves, others with flowers anything from white through green to deepest burgundy red. The flowers are about 2.5cm (1in) across, at the tops of branching narrow stems with deeply cut leaves. They are surrounded by a sun-ray of papery, pointed bracts, the natural form being a pinkish green colour with pale pink centres. One of our oldest cottage-garden plants.

Height: 1m (3ft).

Habitat: Meadows and scrubland, mainly on chalky soil. Does well in partial shade.

Garden care: Water in well when planting and again if the weather turns hot and dry. Keep watch for slugs, especially in spring, when the new shoots are emerging from the ground, and stake in exposed situations.

Propagation: Plants and seed are available from garden centres and nurseries. Seed can be saved from existing plants in the garden and sown in pots or trays in the spring. Plants can be lifted and divided every three years or so in spring or autumn.

Melilot – Ribbed   *Melilotus officinalis*

Also known as the common melilot, this upright, branching biennial has long racemes of yellow pea-like flowers and leaves like a pointed version of clover, with finely toothed edges. It flowers from June to September, the flowers being followed by small, pea-like pods which ripen to black in autumn. There are two closely related species that also grow wild in Britain. The tall melilot (*M. altissima*) looks very similar, but the flowers are darker and the pods hairy. This is found generally in scrub and woodland borders on chalky soil in southern England. The white melilot (*M. alba*) is smaller and found in similar habitats to the ribbed melilot, but has white flowers and is attractive to bees. Where space allows, these plants will grow into bush-like clumps, liberally decorated with the slender spikes of flowers throughout the summer. A very decorative and unusual addition to the mixed flower border.

Height: 1m (3ft).

Habitat: Field edges, waste land and roadsides.

Garden care: Cutting back quite hard towards the end of the flowering season, as with many biennials, can allow you to keep the plant for another year or two.

Propagation: Seed is available from a few specialist nurseries. As for other biennials, it should be sown in pots or trays, outside, in summer, the plants overwintered and then placed where they are to flower in the following spring. Seed can be saved from existing plants.

Mignonette – Wild   *Reseda lutea*

Similar in appearance to garden mignonette (*R. odorata*), which comes originally from North Africa, wild mignonette lacks the rich scent of its garden relative, but is still useful as a subtle backing to plants such as thymes or speedwells in the mixed border or rockery. It is an upright plant with greyish-green leaves finely cut into linear segments, and greenish-yellow flowers in long racemes from May to October. Weld (*R. luteola*) is a closely related plant, similar in appearance and habitat, but larger and with undivided lanceolate leaves and a longer inflorescence. Weld grows as a biennial, whereas mignonette is a short-lived perennial.

Height: 60cm (24in).

Habitat: Roadsides, waste ground and grassy slopes. Often on disturbed ground, especially on chalk or limestone in the south and east of England.

Garden care: Choose a sunny spot, add lime if the soil is acid and dead-head regularly as the flower spikes finish.

Propagation: Available from some specialist nurseries as seed. Sow where it is to flower in mid to late summer, rake in lightly and water well, then leave it to its own devices. Seed can be saved from existing plants and sown in the same way.

Monkshood
Aconitum napellus

By far the most common of our two native monkshoods, the other being *A. anglicum*, a rare plant of south-west England with lilac-blue flowers in May and June. Monkshood is also called wolfsbane for the poison that was extracted from its roots and used to tip the arrows of hunters in the Middle Ages and before. The glossy leaves of this familiar garden plant are dark green, fan-shaped and deeply divided. The flowers, displayed from June into August on branching spikes, are deep blue and hooded. A handsome plant, reminiscent of the delphinium, to which it is related. White- and pink-flowered varieties are also available for the garden. All parts of the plant are poisonous, so it is best to wear gloves when handling it, just to be on the safe side.

Height: 1m (3ft).

Habitat: Damp woods and stream-sides, up to quite high altitudes. Can tolerate sun or shade, but needs some moisture in the soil.

Garden care: Water in well when planting and ensure that it does not dry out in summer. Dead-head as flower spikes become spent, then cut down to ground level in late autumn. A mulch of well-rotted garden compost or farmyard manure at this time of year will be well received by the plant, but is not essential.

Propagation: Plants and seed are available from nurseries and garden centres. Seed can be saved from existing plants and sown in pots outside in late summer. Plants can be lifted and divided in spring or autumn, every three years or so.

Nettle-leaved Bellflower
Campanula trachelium

When not in flower this upright, hairy plant looks very like a nettle. It can grow to 1m (3ft) tall, but often settles for half that or less, especially in a good, sunny situation. The lower leaves have longer stalks than the upper ones, all are triangular in shape and double-toothed like a nettle, and the stiff stems are angular in section. But with the arrival of mid-summer, identification suddenly becomes easy, for the flower buds, held in loose, terminal and near-terminal panicles, begin to open. The flowers are a rich blue, with the classic bell shape of the campanulas and up to 4cm (1.5in) long, opening from late June to September, when they furnish a handsome contrast to some of the hotter colours prominent in the summer garden. The plant grows well, for instance, with yellow loosestrife (*Lysimachia vulgaris*) and bloody cranesbill (*Geranium sanguineum*).

Height: 1m (3ft).

Habitat: Deciduous woodland, hedges and scrub. Tolerant of sun or shade, though it prefers drier soils.

Garden care: Cut back flower spikes when they have finished to encourage further flowering. Cut back to ground level in late autumn. A mulch with bark chippings, leaf mould or well-rotted manure after cutting back at the end of the season is welcome.

Propagation: Plants are available from garden centres. Existing plants can be lifted and divided every three years in spring or autumn. Seed can be saved and sown in pots or trays outside in summer, though they will not germinate until after a significant cold spell, such as they would naturally experience through the winter.

Sea Holly

Eryngium maritimum

This branched perennial, along with its more slender and more-branched cousin field holly (*Eryngo E. campestre*), grows from a basal rosette of smooth-edged, long, slim, ovoid leaves. The stem leaves, however, are vastly different. Stiff, curled and with many large spines around the edge, these are what give the sea holly its name. The stems begin to rise in spring, growing and branching and eventually forming rosettes of spines at their tips, in the centres of which are formed the flower heads, rounded or oval, up to 5cm (2in) long and usually bluish in colour when they open from July to September. A spectacular statement in the border.

Height: 30–60cm (12–24in).

Habitat: Sandy soils, dunes and shingle beaches, usually on the coast, though it will thrive in any well-drained neutral or alkaline soil. Likes full sun.

Garden care: Water in when planting but should not need further watering. Cut back stems to ground level in late autumn.

Propagation: Plants and seed are available from garden centres and nurseries, along with several introduced species. Plants can be lifted and divided every three years or so, but only very carefully, for they do not like root disturbance.

Self-heal

Prunella vulgaris

The squarish stems of this perennial herb, often a pinkish-green colour, rise from short rhizomes. They bear light-green elliptical leaves in widely spaced pairs, one pair of which is found tight to the base of the short flower spike. All of the flowers in any spike will never be found to be out at once. Self-heal forms a thick clump of buds, seed heads and open, hooded flowers, very similar to those of the mints and sages, to which it is related. Very variable in size, according to where it is growing, the self-heal has long been cultivated in gardens, and there are white-flowered and variegated-leaved varieties available as well as the natural violet-flowered type.

Height: 5–35cm (2–14in), depending on competition for light and moisture as well as grazing or clipping.

Habitat: Meadows, scrubland and woods. Will grow in sun or shade, on damp or dry ground.

Garden care: Water in well when planting, but watering should not be needed after the plant has settled. Dead-head when a spike is fully over. Look out for blackspot on the leaves and pick off affected ones, burning them or throwing them in the dustbin.

Propagation: Plants and seed are available from nurseries and garden centres. Seed can be saved from existing plants and sown in pots in late summer. Plants can be lifted and divided every three or four years.

Sheep's-bit
Jasione montana

Despite the fact that it looks like a scabious and is sometimes called sheep's scabious, this is not a scabious. Instead it is classified as a member of the bellflower family. It has a rosette of toothed, narrow leaves from which several almost leafless flowering stems rise in late spring. The tiny deep-blue flowers, clustered into scabious-like button heads about 4cm (1.5in) across, open from June to August. A perennial plant, it looks very pretty in the sun at the front of a border, combined with one of the knapweeds or poppies.

Height: Up to 60cm (24in), but often much smaller, depending on how much competition for light it has.

Habitat: Dry grassland, cliff tops and the edges of pine woods. Can tolerate neutral to alkaline soils. Prefers some moisture, but not too much.

Garden care: Water in well when planting and again if the weather turns hot and dry for an extended period. Dead-head to extend the flowering period. Mulch in autumn with well-rotted garden compost or manure. Stake if grown tightly among other plants, so that it grows tall.

Propagation: Plants and seed are available from specialist nurseries and occasionally some garden centres. Seed can be saved from existing plants and sown in pots outside in autumn to germinate in the following spring.

Speedwell – Spiked
Veronica spicata

Although this is by far the most commonly grown species of native speedwell in our gardens, it is the rarest in the wild and, as such, is a protected species. There are many varieties which have been bred for the garden, varying from white through pale and dark blues to pink and even dark-red flowers, though the natural form has sky-blue blooms from June to August. It has long, rounded leaves, opposite on the stem and downy with toothed edges. These get smaller as they get higher up the stem towards the base of the long, slender flower spike, of which there can be several to a plant. The flowers are tiny but too numerous to count, the spike thick and up to 30cm (12in) long.

Height: 60cm (24in).

Habitat: Pastures, sunny slopes and rocky places, usually in milder regions.

Garden care: Once established in a warm, sunny site, little care is needed. Dead-head when flower spikes are spent and mulch in spring or autumn.

Propagation: Plants and seed are available from nurseries and some garden centres. Existing plants can be lifted and divided in spring or autumn.

St John's Wort

Hypericum sp.

There are around four hundred species of St John's wort, distributed from Ireland to Japan. Some are shrubby, like the European and Chinese introductions commonly used in our gardens; others are evergreen herbs; still others are herbaceous perennials, as Britain's fourteen native species tend to be. Of these, common or perforate St John's wort (*H. perforatum*) is probably the most widespread, growing from England's south coast to the Scottish Highlands. It is distinguished by having clear, translucent spots, filled with oil, on the long, oval leaves, and black spots on the petals and flower stalks. It grows up to 1m (3ft) tall, with many leafy branches and the flowers, up to 2.5cm (1in) across, are borne in terminal branched clumps from June to September.

Square-stalked St John's wort (*H. tetrapterum*), pictured, is up to 60cm (24in) high, with more oblong leaves, no spotting and larger, fewer flowers. It tends to grow in damp places. Trailing St John's wort (*H. humifusum*) is a small, trailing plant, the stems rarely more than 15cm (6in) long, whose flowers do not open in bad weather. It is often found on acid heaths, along with slender St John's wort (*H. pulchrum*), which is a larger plant, up to 60cm (24in) tall. Taller again, at around 1m (3ft), and an acid hater like the common species, is hairy St John's wort (*H. hirsutum*), which has hairs on both sides of the small, narrow leaves and pale-yellow flowers through July and August. This species tends to be found in damp woodland and scrub.

So it can be seen from these few examples that there is a St John's wort for most situations in the garden, bringing their bright-yellow flowers with prominent bunches of pretty stamens throughout the summer months.

Height: Most species grow to 30–100cm (12–36in), with the exception of the trailing one, which rarely exceeds 15cm (6in) and is ideal for a rockery or container.

Habitat: Each has its own niche: some like wet ground, some dry; some acid, some limy. Check specific details when making your selection, but be assured of finding one to suit your situation.

Garden care: Choose a species which suits the spot you wish to place it in, water in well when planting, dead-head thoroughly to prolong flowering and cut down stems of herbaceous species in late autumn. An organic mulch in winter will help give vigour to the plants in the following year. Plants can contract fungal diseases, such as black spot or rust, and affected leaves should be removed and destroyed as soon as this is noticed.

Propagation: Native species are available from nurseries as plants or seed. Seed should be sown in pots or trays outside, the plants placed into their flowering positions in late spring. Cuttings can be taken in summer and rooted in pots of compost, sealed into a plastic bag.

Toadflax – Common   *Linaria vulgaris*

This usually 30cm (12in) perennial has bright-yellow, snap-dragon-like flowers with a long, nectar-filled spur on the back of the lower lip. These are carried in a short spike at the top of the slim stem. Narrow grey-green leaves grow up the stem to the base of the flower spike. The flowering season extends from June to October and, like many plants, can be extended by dead-heading. Toadflax enjoys sun, but is strong enough to withstand close competition in a short-cropped meadow environment. A tight bunch of it would also look excellent on a rockery, perhaps with heartsease and a gentian or soapwort.

Height: 60cm (24in)

Habitat: Short grassland, roadside verges and field edges.

Garden care: Grow in full sun for best results. Partial shade can be tolerated, but the plants tend to be taller and weaker.

Propagation: As with its multi-coloured foreign relatives, best sown where it is to flower, either in autumn or early spring. Each plant will spread a little by underground rhizomes, but seed is easy to collect once you have the plants. Plants and seed are available from specialist nurseries. Garden centres tend to stock the very similar but multi-coloured foreign varieties, which are annuals.

Viper's Bugloss

Echium vulgare

Named for the shape of its seeds, this hairy member of the borage family has a close relative that comes originally from the Canary Islands, but can be seen in gardens and sometimes in the wild in Cornwall and grows to 4.2m (14ft) high. Our native bugloss, however, is of more manageable size, growing up to 1m (3ft), over half of which is taken up by the long flower spike from early June to late September. The plant grows as a biennial, producing in the first year a rosette of dark-green, 20cm (8in) leaves covered with stiff hairs. In the second year a bristly stem rises, with smaller leaves growing ladder-wise from it, getting smaller as they near the top. It is from the axils of these that the flowers come. These are red in bud opening to a rich blue with prominent reddish stamens, each flower a 2cm (0.75in) bell with an irregular lip. These are attractive to bees, moths and butterflies. If the plant is allowed to seed it will die.

Height: 1m (3ft).

Habitat: Open dry grassland and downs, waste ground, quarries and beach heads, mostly in the south of England. Likes dry ground, sunshine and chalky or limestone soils.

Garden care: Water in well when planting, give the plant space and light and cut down the flowering stems promptly when they have finished in order to keep the plant for another year. When handling the plant wear gloves, as it has many tiny, hair-like spines which it will readily leave in your fingers.

Propagation: Seed and plants are available from nurseries. Seed can be saved from existing plants, but this will mean the sacrifice of those plants.

MIXED BORDERS

	HEIGHT	FLOWERING SEASON	FLOWER COLOUR
Bistort – Common	60cm (24in)	May–Aug	Pink
Celandine – Lesser	15cm (6in)	Feb–May	Yellow
Chives	25cm (10in)	May–July	Pink
Columbine	50cm (20in)	May–June	Blue/pink/white
Cranesbill – Bloody	30cm (12in)	May–Sept	Pink
Feverfew	45cm (18in)	July–Oct	White
Fumitory	30cm (12in)	May–Sept	Pink
Grape Hyacinth	22cm (9in)	April–May	Blue
Harebell	50cm (20in)	June–Sept	Blue
Jacob's Ladder	60cm (24in)	May–Aug	Blue
Lady's Mantle	45cm (18in)	May–Sept	Yellow
Mallow – Common	1m (3ft)	June–Sept	Mauve
Mallow – Musk	1m (3ft)	June–Aug	Pink
Marjoram	60cm (24in)	June–Sept	Pink
Masterwort	1m (3ft)	June–July	White/pink
Melilot – Ribbed	1m (3ft)	June–Sept	Yellow
Mignonette – Wild	60cm (24in)	May–Oct	Yellow
Monkshood	1m (3ft)	June–Aug	Blue
Nettle-leaved Bellflower	1m (3ft)	June–Sept	Blue
Sea Holly	60cm (24in)	July–Sept	Blue
Self-heal	35cm (14in)	June–Sept	Blue
Sheep's-bit	60cm (24in)	June–Aug	Blue
Speedwell – Spiked	60cm (24in)	June–Aug	Blue
St John's Wort	1m (3ft)	June–Sept	Yellow
Toadflax – Common	60cm (24in)	June–Oct	Yellow
Viper's Bugloss	1m (3ft)	June–Sept	Blue

Chapter Two

Rockery and Wall Plants

ROCKERY AND WALL PLANTS

Y OU DO not need to build a rockery in order to enjoy rockery plants. Indeed, you do not even need a sunny site, as several are very tolerant of shade. Any free-draining position will do, however restricted the root-run. The cracks between the slabs of a patio are ideal, especially for plants that give off scent when trodden on or brushed past, like feverfew (*Tanacetum parthenium*), chamomile (*Anthemis nobile*) or the thymes. Mosses, stonecrops, navelwort (*Umbilicus rupestris*) or Welsh poppies (*Meconopsis cambrica*) can gain the tiniest of footholds in the crevices of an old wall. An increasingly popular way of enlarging potential plant space is to leave a planting channel in the top of a garden wall. Many of the plants mentioned in this chapter and some others would be

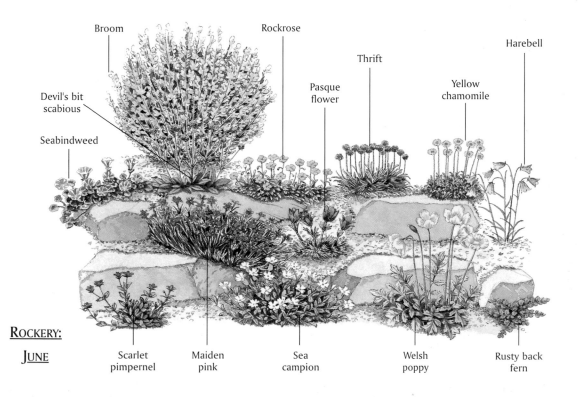

ROCKERY:

JUNE

Broom · Rockrose · Harebell · Thrift · Pasque flower · Yellow chamomile · Devil's bit scabious · Seabindweed · Scarlet pimpernel · Maiden pink · Sea campion · Welsh poppy · Rusty back fern

A scarlet pimpernel

perfectly happy in such a position. A drive through the lanes of Cornwall or West Wales will reveal some of the more incongruous-seeming possibilities for plants that will tolerate and even thrive in the free-draining, sunny conditions of the classic rockery situation.

The rockery is something that was overdone and often badly done in the 1960s and 1970s, so that now it is distinctly out of fashion. The trick with a rockery is to make it look as if it belongs. If you are building a new one, then choose local stone, study what you get to find its natural grain so that you can lay it the right way, then bury most of it in the soil. That soil should be mixed liberally with grit

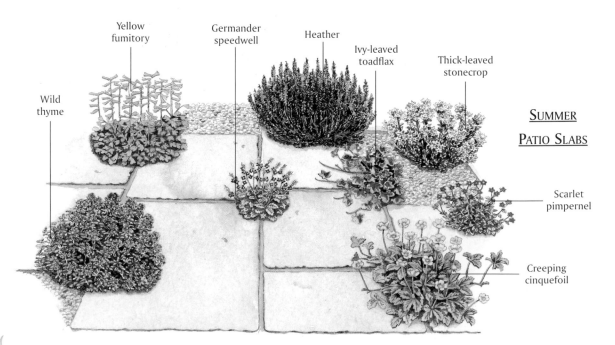

Yellow fumitory

Germander speedwell

Heather

Ivy-leaved toadflax

Thick-leaved stonecrop

Wild thyme

SUMMER PATIO SLABS

Scarlet pimpernel

Creeping cinquefoil

or sand, if not both. And then visit any local outcrops of rock, cliffs, long-abandoned quarries, ruins or sand-banks to check out the must-haves growing in your area. These can then give the basis for a wider-ranging planting scheme, as you know that they will thrive in your conditions. Then comes the fun part – choosing the plants that you really want. Do not buy anything 'just to fill a gap', as you can be sure that something will fill it for you by next year. Think about shapes, textures, leaf types and flowering times. It is not something that design students are willing to admit, but it is very difficult to achieve a plant combination that clashes, so do not worry about that.

Whether you are building a new rockery, creating a raised bed, adding interest to a wall or patio or filling a few tubs or troughs, all these situations are ideally suited to rockery plants – indeed, more so than to the petunias, lobelia, pelargoniums and so on that are normally found in containers. As long as the plants you choose are happy, you will be rewarded with a lovely display in the colour combinations of your choice. And with the right plant choices, that display can go on from February right through to October.

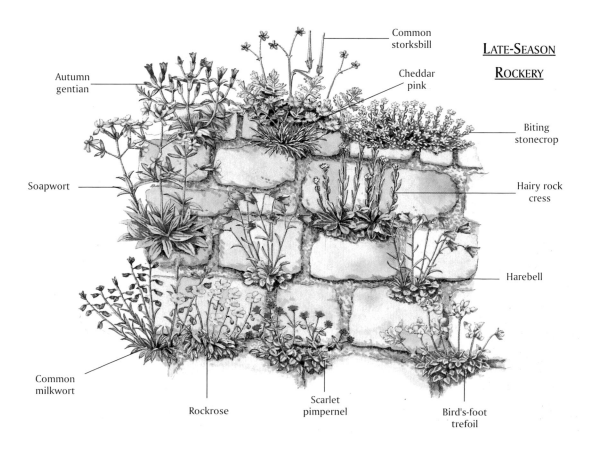

LATE-SEASON ROCKERY

Common storksbill

Cheddar pink

Autumn gentian

Biting stonecrop

Soapwort

Hairy rock cress

Harebell

Common milkwort

Rockrose

Scarlet pimpernel

Bird's-foot trefoil

Bellflower – Creeping

Campanula patula

Closely related to the harebell and the other bellflowers, the creeping bellflower is not common in the wild, but has found a niche in our gardens. Its open, pale-blue, five-petalled flowers are about 2.5cm (1in) across and fairly cover the plant for about three months at the height of summer. Of all the bellflowers, it is most similar in appearance to the harebell, with its pale flowers, slender stems and tight, long buds. Also the leaves are similar, the basal leaves stalked and spoon-shaped while those further up the lax stems are narrow and lanceolate. The plant will spread to form quite substantial mats of foliage if allowed and will self-seed freely.

Height: 60cm (24in).

Habitat: Meadows, waste ground and scrub.

Garden care: Once planted and watered in, it should not need further watering in the garden, but will, of course, in containers. Excessive growth can simply be pulled or clipped away to keep the plant within the bounds you have allowed in the garden.

Propagation: Plants and seed are available from garden centres and nurseries. Seed can be saved from plants in the garden or allowed to distribute itself and the young plants transplanted to where they are required. Clumps can be lifted and divided every two or three years.

Bird's-foot Trefoil   *Lotus corniculatus*

A pretty little plant with bright-yellow, pea-like flowers about 1cm (0.5in) long, reddish when in bud. It can happily hug the ground on footpaths, growing no more than 2.5cm (1in) high, or it can attain 35cm (14in) in longer grass, where it tends to grow in the company of plants such as sainfoin and ox-eye daisy. It looks trifoliate, but in fact there are five lobes to each leaf, three of them at the end of a short stalk, the other two at its base. The name comes from the fruit, which is 2cm (0.75in) long, chestnut brown when ripe and spread out like a bird's foot. The flowers appear from May until the autumn frosts, but mainly in June and July.

Height: Varies from 2.5–35cm (1–14in), depending on situation.

Habitat: Dry grassland, meadows and footpaths.

Garden care: Provide well-drained, sunny aspect and this plant will look after itself either as a specimen on the rockery or in a meadow situation.

Propagation: Scarification, or scratching, of the seed helps germination, as with all the pea family. Seed can then be broadcast or sown in pots for later transplantation.

Campion – Sea

Silene uniflora

Often regarded as a sub-species of the erect, 60cm (24in) bladder campion (*S. vulgaris*) of roadsides and downland, with its white flowers backed by broad, ovoid bladders, the sea campion is very similar but much shorter, with fleshier leaves and a low, cushion-shaped habit. The branching stems of both types are greyish in colour, the narrow ovoid leaves greyish green, as are the bladder-like calices behind the flowers, though these are sometimes pinkish white. The flowers of the sea campion, about 2cm (0.75in) across, are often borne singly on their slender stems, unlike those of the bladder campion, which are in loose bunches on stems that divide repeatedly into threes. These plants will flower all through the summer from May to September and will grow in the poorest of conditions.

Height: 15cm (6in).

Habitat: Cliff tops and ledges, shingle and short grassland.

Garden care: Water in when planting, choosing a sunny site. Dead-head regularly to keep the plant looking tidy.

Propagation: Seed and plants are available from nurseries and garden centres. Seed can be saved towards the end of the flowering season and sown in gritty compost in pots or trays outside or where the plants are required.

Centaury – Common

Centaurium erythraea

Although it has a similar name to the knapweeds, this pink-flowered biennial is more closely related to the gentians. Its smooth, light-green stems rise from a basal rosette of oval leaves and bear shiny, pointed elliptical leaves in pairs, up to the point where they branch into a loose umbel-like arrangement to be topped by the starry, yellow-centred pink flowers. The flowering season is from July to September. Like many plants, the common centaury is very variable in size, according to its growing conditions. Competition for light and moisture can create a plant anything from 5–45cm (2–18in) high, with one or many stems, but however large it gets, the flowers are a pretty sight in the sun and it makes a good companion to more substantial plants, such as the knapweeds, campions or geraniums.

Height: To 45cm (18in).

Habitat: Dry meadows and grassy slopes. Sunny sites.

Garden care: In common with some other biennials, plants can be saved for another year of flowering if they are not allowed to set seed.

Propagation: Sow seeds in summer and overwinter plants in pots for planting out in spring or in their flowering position. Plants and seed are available from specialist nurseries.

Cinquefoil – Creeping

Potentilla reptans

Bright yellow, five-petalled flowers up to 2.5cm (1in) across stand up to 7cm (2.75in) above the ground-hugging, strawberry-like leaves of this trailing sun-lover. The stems stretch up to 22cm (9in) across the ground, rooting occasionally at the leaf axils, leaves and flowers being borne in groups along the stem. The compound leaves, made of five centrally attached, toothed leaflets, give the plant its common name from the Norman French. A good plant for trailing over rocks or as a filler between other low-growing plants with a contrasting flower colour, such as scarlet pimpernell. Similar in flower colour, size, flowering season and habitat is the four-petalled tormentil (*P. erecta*). More inclined to be erect and tufted, it also makes a very good rockery subject, though it will not thrive on calcareous soils.

Height: 5–10cm (2–4in).

Habitat: Banks and roadsides in short grassland.

Garden care: Stems can be cut back in autumn after flowering has finished to keep the plant tidy. The leaves, especially if growing in shade or damp conditions, can contract a brown rust disease. If caught early this can be treated by removal and destruction of the affected leaves. Otherwise a fungicide spray will be necessary.

Propagation: Seed and plants are available from specialist nurseries. Once established, pegging down the stems at intervals will encourage stem rooting, after which new plants can be cut away and moved to where they are required.

Cranesbill – Dove's-foot

Geranium molle

Small pink flowers roughly 2cm (0.75in) across adorn this annual through June and July, sitting in pairs or singly above shallowly cut, almost-round leaves. It is one of three common annual cranesbills native to these shores, probably the most common of which is the cut-leaved cranesbill (*G. dissectum*), found on arable land and grassland in southern Britain. This has deeply divided leaves and darker, more cerise-coloured petals. The third of the common annual species is the small-flowered cranesbill (*G. pusillum*), whose leaves fall somewhere between the other two species in appearance, the flowers similar in colour to the cut-leaved geranium, but with a whitish centre. Dove's-foot cranesbill flowers from April to September, the others from May to August. All make a good contrast when combined with larger-flowered species of similar colour in a tub or basket, as long as they are dead-headed regularly.

Height: 30cm (12in).

Habitat: All grow in meadow land, on roadsides and dry banks.

Garden care: These are fairly insignificant plants if grown on their own, but are ideal fillers in summer schemes, for instance between plants of bloody cranesbill, pink pansies or contrasting white or blue flowers like Bladder Campion (*Silene vulgaris*) or Sea Lavender (*Limonium vulgare*). Among non-natives, a good combination would be with pink petunias.

Propagation: Although only small plants, the annual cranesbills produce quite large seeds, which need scarification, or scratching, to aid germination. They are hardy, so can be sown in autumn or spring. Seed is available from specialist nurseries.

Daisy
Bellis perennis

A wonderful example of the perversity of British gardeners. As children, we enjoy their bright, summery white-petalled flowers, born singly on hairy stalks above rosettes of spoon-shaped leaves with thick, flattened stems. We appreciate the delicate pink of the backs of the petal tips as they close in the evening. Then, as adults, we spend hours trying to eradicate them from our lawns, only to go to the local garden centre or market and buy cultivated varieties of them to edge our borders and window boxes in the spring.

The native plant can flower all year, but mainly from April to July. The cultivated varieties of it – some pink, some red, some semi-double, others fully double with the yellow centre completely hidden in a pompom of bright petals – are grown as biennials and flower over the same period.

Height: 7cm (2.75in).

Habitat: Short grassland.

Garden care: Ideal plant for the rockery. Also suited to border edging and container planting in sun or partial shade.

Propagation: Sow seed in early summer and overwinter plants for flowering the following year, or lift and divide plants in spring. Commercial varieties are widely available in spring as plants. Seed of the native species is available from specialist nurseries or plants from most lawns.

Heartsease
Viola tricolor

This extremely variable little flower is the parent of all those hundreds of different pansies which are sold from every outlet imaginable throughout Britain all through the year. Of itself it has small flowers, maybe 2.5cm (1in) or so tall by 2cm (0.75in) across, sometimes all yellow, sometimes yellow and white or yellow and purple, sometimes with stripes radiating from the centre, sometimes not. In all these combinations, it is a sprawling plant with fairly lax stems and mid-green leaves often held in bunches from the stem. The lower leaves are rounded and heart-shaped with toothed edges, while the upper leaves are longer, narrowing towards the base. The plant flowers from April to September. There is a very similar species, the field pansy (*V. arvensis*), the flowers of which tend to be mainly white or pale yellow.

Height: 5–45cm (2–18in).

Habitat: Field edges, scrubland, meadows and rocky places all provide this little plant with homes. Can thrive in sun or light shade.

Garden care: Dead-heading will keep the plants flowering through the season, instead of in 'fits and starts'. Cut back stems when they get straggly and at the end of the flowering season. Water when the weather remains hot and dry for an extended period.

Propagation: Seed and plants are available from specialist nurseries. If cultivated pansies are allowed to seed, some will revert to the species type. Cuttings can be taken in summer and potted up with a plastic bag over the top to retain moisture.

Navelwort
Umbilicus rupestris

Also known as wall pennywort, this shade-tolerant perennial is often found on walls and rocky banks, especially where there is a source of moisture. Its roots can penetrate deep into the cracks of a wall to draw out any water for the smooth, fleshy round leaves and short spike of drooping creamy-green flowers. The leaves are about the size of an old penny (giving it its alternate name) with a dimple in the centre where the stem attaches to the underside. They are often quite pale. The flower stem is reddish, the flowers appearing from June to August. After setting seed, the plant withers and turns to a reddish-brown colour, then dies back fully into its thick, rhizomatous root until early in the following spring.

Height: 30cm (12in).

Habitat: Old walls, steep banks and cliff faces, especially in or on the edge of woodland. Tolerates sun or shade.

Garden care: Surprisingly hardy plant. Once established, needs little maintenance. Simply tidy up dead leaves and flower stems in autumn.

Propagation: Seed and plants are available from nurseries and a few garden centres. If planting in the cracks of a rock face, probably best done as a seed, or pinch of seeds. Plants can be placed in more easily worked sites. Water in well after planting.

Pasque Flower
Pulsatilla vulgaris

Named in Norman French for Easter, which is when it flowers, this is one of our most beautiful native flowers and now a rare one in the wild. It is widely used in gardens, both in the natural purplish mauve colour and in cultivated white and red forms. Much-divided, soft, feathery grey leaves form a basal rosette which is almost evergreen, dying back in late summer or autumn to reappear in winter. From the centre of this arise hairy stems, each with a single bud at its apex, above a whorl of leaves. When the cup-shaped flowers open, from March to May, they can be seen to contain a large boss of bright-yellow stamens, surrounding a dark-purple stigma. Later, the flowers are replaced by wildly hairy seed heads, similar to those of some clematis species, giving away the close relationship between the two. An essential for any garden, especially one on neutral or limy soil.

Height: 10–30cm (4–12in).

Habitat: Dry grassland on alkaline soils, such as the South Downs of southern England.

Garden care: Ensure that the soil is not acidic before attempting to grow this plant. Then firm it in well in a sunny spot. Tidy up the leaves when they die back and cut back most of the seed heads if you do not require the seed, thus saving the plant's energy for growing.

Propagation: Plants and seed are available from garden centres and nurseries. Seed can be saved from plants in the garden and sown in pots in summer.

Pimpernel – Scarlet   *Anagallis arvensis*

Orangy salmon-red, rather than scarlet, the flowers of this tiny plant are five-petalled, with bright-yellow dots on the ends of the stamens, and about 2cm (0.75in) across. Scarlet pimpernel is an annual with squarish, creeping stems which occasionally throw up erect, leafy side branches. The leaves are stalkless, pointed ovals, born in opposite pairs. The flowers, which close at night or when rain is approaching, are on long, leafless stalks. There are several garden cultivars, probably the most popular of which is a large-flowered, dark-blue variety though there are pink and lilac ones, too. It has a close relative, the blue pimpernel (*A. foemina*) which unsurprisingly has blue flowers and another, the bog pimpernel (*A. tenella*), with pink flowers, which is found naturally in wetlands and short damp grassland in the West Country of England, Wales, Ireland and Scotland. The yellow pimpernel (*Lysimachia nemorum*) is actually related to the loosestrifes. Scarlet pimpernel and its cultivars make excellent subjects for the rockery or hanging basket.

Height: Up to 10cm (4in), but commonly half that.

Habitat: Short grassland, cliff tops and field edges.

Garden care: A tough little customer, this relative of the primrose needs little attention, apart from watering in well when planting and until established and dead-heading through the flowering season, which lasts from June to October.

Propagation: Seed is available from nurseries. Garden cultivars are available as plants or seed from some garden centres and nurseries. Seed can be saved in late summer or autumn and sown fresh where it is to flower, in pots or trays outside, to be planted out in tubs or baskets in the spring.

Pineappleweed

Matricaria matricarioides

Closely related to the daisy-like mayweeds, this little plant was probably originally an introduction, though there is disagreement as to from where and when. However, with an almost worldwide distribution, this is not totally surprising. It has finely cut leaves, pale green, as are the branching stems. The conical yellowish flower heads, with no ray florets around them as in other daisies, are about 1cm (0.3in) across and smell of pineapples when crushed. They appear from May to July and, though not the showiest of flowers, make a good counterpoint to some of the less subtle ones, such as daisies (*Bellis perennis*) or thrift (*Armeria maritima*).

Height: 7–30cm (2.75–12in).

Habitat: Arable land, waste ground, pathways and roadsides. Thrives best in sun and on drier ground.

Garden care: Dead-head regularly to extend the flowering season and make the plants bushier for the rest of the season.

Propagation: Seed is available from some specialist nurseries or can be saved from plants already in the garden. Sow fresh each year in pots of moist compost or where they are to flower.

Pink – Maiden   *Dianthus deltoides*

Closely related to another native perennial, the Cheddar pink (*D. gratianopolitanus*), which is a rarity of south-western England, as well as to the border carnations and sweet Williams, the maiden pink supposedly got its name from the cheeks of blushing maidens. The dark stems with their small, lanceolate leaves form dense evergreen mats in many a cottage garden or rockery throughout these islands and beyond. There are several cultivated varieties available with different flower colours – white, pink or red – all of them carrying a dense covering of 2cm (0.75in), five-petalled flowers from June until the autumn.

Height: Up to about 45cm (18in), though usually much less.

Habitat: Likes open, dry soils, neutral to alkaline and a sunny aspect, but can also do well in clay soil, if grit or organic matter is dug in before planting.

Garden care: Dead-head regularly to extend and intensify flowering. Clip back at the end of the season.

Propagation: Seed and plants are available from garden centres and nurseries. Seed can be saved from plants already in the garden. Also cuttings can be taken in summer – literally pulling off non-flowering stems if you can find them and potting up in compost or placing them in a jar of water, where they will root almost as readily.

Rockrose

Helianthemum nummularium

In fact, there are three species of rockrose native to Britain, the other two being the hoary rockrose (*H. canum*) and the white rockrose (*H. apenninum*), but this is the most common both in the wild and in gardens. It is extremely popular and has been cultivated to give many different flower colours, as well as the natural bright yellow. It is really a tiny evergreen shrub with small, linear, dark-green leaves carried in opposite pairs on the sprawling, slender stems, which are often a reddish colour. It has five-petalled flowers, like miniature roses with many stamens, which are borne from May to September.

Height: Up to 30cm (12in).

Habitat: Dry grassland and rocky areas. Acid soil and excessive moisture are not agreeable to the plant, but full sun is important.

Garden care: Dead-head regularly through the flowering season to keep it going, then cut back trailing stems in the autumn to keep the plant bushy.

Propagation: Plants are available in a wide range of flower colours from garden centres and nurseries. Cuttings can be taken and potted up outside in the summer.

Saxifrage – Mossy

Saxifraga hypnoides

There are sixteen different species of saxifrages – or 'stone breakers' as the name translates – growing wild in Britain, almost all having either yellow or white flowers. The mossy saxifrage is one of the white-flowered species and is commonly grown in gardens for its moss-like mounds of finely divided, dark-green leaves, which can form extensive mats if not trimmed back every now and then. For several weeks in spring it covers itself with starry, white, five-petalled flowers about 2cm (0.75in) across.

Height: 7.5–22cm (3–9in).

Habitat: Rocky places and stream-sides in mountainous areas. Can take wet or dry conditions, sun or semi-shade.

Garden care: Dead-head to extend flowering season and keep the plant tidy. Lift and divide clumps every two or three years in spring or autumn to keep to size and make new plants.

Propagation: Plants are available from garden centres and nurseries. Seed available from some specialist nurseries, or can be saved from existing plants.

Scabious – Devil's Bit   *Succisa pratensis*

The scabious family are close relatives of the teasels, but on a very different scale. This dainty little plant has blue or bluish-purple flower heads about 2cm (0.75in) across, in the form of a tight ball with a flattened base, each on the end of its own slim, softly hairy stem. The slender leaves are in a rough basal rosette, with sometimes a few up the stalks. The scabious family take their name from the skin disease scabies, which the juice of the field scabious was used to cure. And why devil's bit? The plant got its name because the thick root ends abruptly, rather than tapering away, so it was suggested that the devil had come up from beneath the surface of the

earth and bitten it off for its curative properties.

There is a similar species, the small scabious (*Scabiosa columbaria*), which usually grows on lime-rich soil and has paler blue flowers, more like a miniature scabious flower in form, and divided leaves as opposed to the entire ones of the devil's bit. The two plants are much the same size, though the devil's bit can grow taller. Both enjoy full sun and both flower from July to October. A third, totally unrelated species, the sheep's-bit (*Jasione montana*) looks very similar, though there are several pale-blue flowers to a stem. It flowers from June to August and is a member of the bellflower family.

Height: Up to 60cm (24in), but more usually 15–22cm (6–9in). In exposed situations, will flower at just 7.5cm (3in).

Habitat: Very adaptable, living in fens, meadows, hedgerows and poor grassland. The small scabious prefers an acid-free soil and the sheep's-bit can tolerate some shade: it can sometimes be found in dry pine woods.

Garden care: Choose from the three plants according to your conditions or the preferred colour if giving them a dry, sunny site

with neutral soil, where they will all thrive. Their delicate looks are misleading and little care will be required.

Propagation: Seed and plants are available from specialist nurseries, and plants sometimes from larger garden centres. Seed is easily collected in autumn and is best sown fresh in pots or seed trays. Bellflowers, including the sheep's-bit, need a period of cold before they will germinate, so do not expect germination until spring for this species.

Scurvy Grass
Cochlearia officinalis

A singularly unattractive name for this attractive plant which is by no means related to the grasses, though the leaves contain high levels of vitamin C and therefore do cure scurvy. Scurvy grass is a very variable plant with heart-shaped, mid-green leaves, the veins often highlighted in dark brown. It forms mounds of thick-stemmed foliage in a wide range of habitats. From mid-spring onwards, right through to September, the foliage is fairly well hidden by a profusion of four-petalled white flowers about 1cm (0.3in) across, which are followed by pea-sized seed pods.

Height: Up to 45cm (18in).

Habitat: Very adaptable, scurvy grass will grow in salt marshes, beside mountain streams or on dry roadside banks as well as on cliffs and walls.

Garden care: Dead-heading will maintain the intensity of the flowering through the summer. A liquid feed every two or three weeks in the flowering season will do it good.

Propagation: Seed is available from specialist nurseries. This should be sown in pots or where it is to flower in summer and kept moist to aid germination. Seed can be saved from existing plants in the garden. The plant can be lifted and divided every two or three years in spring or autumn.

Silverweed
Potentilla anserina

This low-growing, creeping perennial can be found brightening roadsides, short grassland, cliff tops and dry banks throughout Britain, as well as most other countries of the world. It will grow on damp clay or dry shingle, in sun or semi-shade, bringing its silvery leaves, which are sub-divided into deeply toothed leaflets and up to 20cm (8in) long, to almost anywhere its seed will carry to. Its bright yellow flowers can be up to almost 2.5cm (1in) across, their five petals slightly darker towards the centre of the flower. They are carried individually on long stalks from late May until August or even September. Like the strawberries, silverweed has over-ground runners up to 45cm (18in) long, which root at the nodes producing new plants, so it can cover quite an area. It looks brilliant in bright sunshine, especially when contrasted with something dark like a heather, or blue like a speedwell. An excellent subject for the rockery or border edge.

Height: 15cm (6in).

Habitat: Just about anywhere, from flood meadows and lake shores to dry clay or even shingle beaches. Also in woodland and common on road verges.

Garden care: Water in well when planting. Dead-head regularly to prolong flowering and cut back runners to confine the plant.

Propagation: Seed and plants are available from some nurseries. Seed can be saved and sown where it is to flower or in pots or trays outside in late summer. Runners can be allowed to root, then the new plants cut away and transplanted to where they are needed.

Speedwell – Germander

Veronica chamaedrys

One of eighteen species of speedwell that grow wild in the United Kingdom, not all of which are native. The bright-blue flowers of this pretty perennial are borne on short spikes up to 20cm (8in) long, depending on growing conditions. Often the spikes are much shorter when it has little competition for light. The leaves are broad, hairy and toothed, the stems having two opposite rows of hairs. The flowers, borne from April to July, have a white 'eye', which gives the plant its other common name of 'bird's-eye', as well as two long, white stamens. Often the uppermost of the four petals has dark-blue veins radiating from its base.

Wood speedwell (*V. montana*) is similar, but the leaves are stalked and the flowers smaller and more lilac in colour, with the stem hairy all round. Common speedwell (*V. officinalis*) is hairy like the wood speedwell, but with unstalked leaves like the germander and lilac flowers. There are also a number of annual species, including buxbaum's speedwell (*V. persica*), which has shiny-green leaves and bright-blue flowers for most of the year. Even wetlands have their own speedwells, the longer-leaved marsh speedwell and water speedwell, discussed in the relevant chapters of this book. Probably the most commonly seen wild form, however, is not a native, having been introduced from the Caucasus. This is the slender speedwell (*V. filiformis*), which has long, creeping stems with small, rounded leaves and bright-blue flowers, and is a common weed of lawns throughout the country. There are numerous tall garden veronicas, bred from foreign species for the mixed border.

Height: Up to 20cm (8in) in a shaded or densely planted situation; more usually 7.5–10cm (3–4in).

Habitat: Hedgerows and grassland. Likes the sun, so makes a very good rockery or border edging plant.

Garden care: Avoid ericaceous soils. Dead-head regularly to extend the flowering season. Clip back creeping stems to keep the plant where it is required.

Propagation: Plants and seed are available from nurseries. Seed can be sown throughout the warmer months in pots or trays of good compost. The plants will spread by creeping stems, which root if given the opportunity. Once established, these can be separated from the parent and replanted where required.

Stonecrop – Biting   *Sedum acre*

One of three yellow-flowered stonecrops native to Britain, this mat-forming perennial is also known as 'wall pepper' for its sharp taste. Its prostrate stems are much-branched and tightly covered with tiny, fleshy oval leaves with a flat upper surface. These usually overlap on the non-flowering stems. The flowers are 1cm (0.5in) across, bright-yellow five-petalled stars with a prominent central boss, a little like the flowers of a hypericum in miniature. They are borne in small bunches, at or near the tips of the stems. The plant will root in the driest of places, even halfway up the side of a stone wall, and can be a little on the invasive side if allowed to spread unchecked. It will spread eventually to about 60cm (24in) across and is covered in flowers from early June until late in August, especially if you have the patience to dead-head it once a week or so. This is a very valuable plant for those places where little else will be tough enough to grow. It can look very pretty in a rockery if you can keep pulling up the seedlings to stop it taking over.

Height: About 10cm (4in). Spread up to 60cm (24in).

Habitat: Dry banks, walls, dunes and among rocks. Likes full sun.

Garden care: If required in those awkward little places, like in a wall, then plant a couple of seeds in the tiniest bit of soil, rather than compost, and water well with a spray. It should germinate in a fairly short time. In easier places, plants can be tucked in and watered, then should take care of themselves. Dead-heading can be done during or after flowering and, though a little fiddly on this scale, is recommended in order to keep the plant from spreading where it is not required.

Propagation: Seed and plants are available from nurseries and some garden centres. Cuttings can be taken in summer from existing plants and rooted in pots of coarse compost.

Stonecrop – English *Sedum anglicum*

One of two white-flowered species of stonecrop native to Britain, this one is found only in the west and is distinguished from its more widespread relative, the white stonecrop (*S. album*), by having smaller leaves that hold tight to the stem and flower stems that are branched only once rather than several times. Found naturally growing over rocks in sunny positions, these plants are ideally suited to the rockery situation or to walls. Their five-petalled flowers are held in profusion above the succulent leaves from May to August in even the driest conditions.

Height: The English stonecrop grows to just 7.5cm (3in); the white stonecrop up to 22cm (9in).

Habitat: Rocks, cliffs and dry places, but will thrive in better conditions if lack of competition allows.

Garden care: The main task with these plants is pruning, as they will spread vigorously if allowed. There is a yellow-flowered and grey-leaved variety of the white stonecrop called 'Coral Carpet' which is available from garden centres and spreads to only 22cm (9in) across – this is much more manageable in a small rockery.

Propagation: Plants and seeds are available from nurseries and garden centres. Cuttings can be taken and rooted in sandy compost in the growing season.

Strawberry – Wild *Fragaria vesca*

With five-petalled white flowers 1–2.5cm (0.5–1in) across from April right through the summer, the wild strawberry is a pretty little plant for the shady side of a rockery, even without the fruit. These are much smaller than the cultivated varieties, which originate in America, but very sweet, with prominent pips. The typically strawberry-like trilobed leaves are mid-green, with bold veining and toothed edges. The strawberry was named for the habit of placing straw beneath the berries to keep the dirt off them in wet weather.

Height: Up to 30cm (12in), but often half that.

Habitat: Hedges, woods and scrubland, often but not always in shade.

Garden care: Ensure that they are planted with the crowns exactly at soil level. Picking the fruit is actually good for the plant, as well as making it produce more, for we tend to pick it before the seeds are actually ripe. Cut back or pot up runners. Keep an eye on the plants for viral disease and, if found, destroy them. There is also a beetle that attacks the roots. If this is found to be a problem, then dig out and discard the surrounding soil, replacing with fresh earth from elsewhere in the garden and planting new strawberries in another spot.

Propagation: Plants and seed are available from nurseries and a few garden centres. Small plants formed on runners can be potted up, then cut free when they have rooted, or fruit can be picked when over-ripe and potted up so that the seed will germinate in the autumn.

Thrift

Armeria maritima

Also known as 'sea pink', this neat little perennial has grassy leaves and pink pompoms of flowers about 2.5cm (1in) across. It is one of the staples of any rock garden, as well as brightening the cliffs and shores of our coastline. The hummocks of foliage are evergreen, spreading to over 30cm (12in) across. The flowers are borne on bare, slender stems up to 15cm (6in) long, in profusion from May to September. Usually they are pink, but there is a white variety seen occasionally in the wild and also available in some garden centres. This plant has been used since ancient times as a pretty path edging and is unendingly popular in gardens across Britain. There is a very pretty variety with variegated leaves occasionally available from garden centres.

Height: Occasionally up to 30cm (12in), but more usually half that.

Habitat: Cliff tops, mountains, salt marshes and shingle. Very well adapted to the need to conserve moisture, the one thing this plant does not enjoy is shade.

Garden care: Water in well when planting, dead-head to extend the flowering season and clip back the main stems to confine it if necessary.

Propagation: Plants are readily available from nurseries and garden centres as well as market stalls and D.I.Y stores in spring, both the pink and the white varieties. Seed is also available from some nurseries. The creeping stems can be cut back and the cuttings trimmed and potted up in gritty compost to root in a few weeks.

Thyme – Wild

Thymus praecox

One of several species of thyme that grow wild in Britain, this small, carpeting aromatic sub-shrub thrives on dry banks, rocky places and even sand dunes. It is tolerant of acid or limy soils and enjoys a sunny aspect. Thymes are invaluable in the kitchen for their aromatic leaves as well as in the garden, where their pinkish flowers will brighten a warm spot in the height of summer. Wild thyme flowers mainly in early summer, but with regular dead-heading will continue through until early autumn. It is a low, spreading plant, achieving a width of anything up to 60cm (24in), but a height of only 10cm (4in) when in flower. The prostrate main stems send up vertical flowering stalks with the characteristic round to oval flower heads at the tops.

Similar species include common thyme (*T. vulgaris*), a shrubby evergreen with dark-green leaves which grows to 30cm (12in) high and flowers throughout the summer. Also broad-leaved or large thyme *(T. pulegioides)*, which also has dark-green leaves and flowers right through the summer, but grows to only 7.5–10cm (3–4in). Breckland thyme (*T. serpyllum*) is rare in the wild, but is the variety most taken to by gardeners. This has narrow, dark-green leaves, darker flowers than the others, a low, creeping habit and again flowers from June to September.

Height: 10cm (4in) when in flower.

Habitat: Dry, sunny places. Grassy banks, limestone pavements, scree and sand dunes.

Garden care: Water in well when planting. Dead-head regularly to prolong the flowering period. Prune to maintain required shape and size.

Propagation: Thymes, both native and imported, are commonly available in garden centres and nurseries, especially in early summer. Almost all are evergreen and can be planted from the pot whenever the weather is not too cold, though they are best planted in summer. Softwood cuttings can be taken during the warmer months and potted in gritty compost to root in a sheltered area.

Vervain

Verbena officinalis

Exquisite little mauve flowers decorate this relative of the garden verbenas, which were bred from imported American species, from June to September. A plant for the front of the border or rockery, where it can be enjoyed from close up, it has undivided, toothed leaves at the base and near the tops of the branching, squarish stems. Between these two areas, the leaves are finely divided, giving a ferny effect. There are coarse hairs on the angles of the stems of this constituent of salves and medicines since at least the days of the Celts, from whom the name comes. The small flowers are borne in long, slender spikes, not all the flowers on a spike being out at the same time.

Height: 30–60cm (12–24in).

Habitat: Dry, stony places such as walls, scree slopes and footpath edges as well as meadows. Will thrive in full sun or partial shade.

Garden care: Water in well when planting, but should not need further watering. Remove flowering spike when it is finished to encourage more spikes and cut back hard at the end of the season.

Propagation: Plants and seed are available from nurseries. Seed can be saved from existing plants in the garden and sown in late summer in pots or trays outside or where it is to flower.

Whitlow-grass – Yellow

Draba aizoides

Rarely has there been a more inappropriate-sounding Latin name given to a plant than *Draba* for this brilliant little gem. Confined in the wild to one small area in south Wales, it is becoming popular in gardens as it becomes better known. The narrow, dark-green evergreen leaves are just 2.5cm (1in) or so long and fringed with bristles, growing in little tufts. The stems are leafless, with bunches of bright, starry little sulphur-yellow flowers at the tops which have rounded petals and many stamens. It begins to flower early, sometimes in March, and continues sporadically until August, the flowers being around 1.5cm (0.5in) across.

Height: Up to about 10cm (4in).

Habitat: Open grassland, scree slopes and rocky areas, often on alkaline soils. Not a moisture-lover, but does need plenty of sun.

Garden care: Place this little perennial where it can be seen and enjoyed from close-up, as it will never be large. Dead-head to extend the flowering season and allow the plant to grow rather than set seeds.

Propagation: Plants and seed are available from good garden centres and nurseries. Seed can be saved from existing plants in the garden or the little leaf rosettes can be cut away and planted up as cuttings in pots in summer.

ROCKERY AND WALL PLANTS

	HEIGHT	FLOWERING SEASON	FLOWER COLOUR
Bellflower – Creeping	60cm (24in)	June–Aug	Blue
Bird's-foot Trefoil	40cm (16in)	May–Oct	Yellow
Campion – Sea	15cm (6in)	May–Sept	White
Centaury – Common	45cm (18in)	July–Sept	Pink
Cinquefoil – Creeping	10cm (4in)	June–Sept	Yellow
Cranesbill – Dove's-foot	30cm (12in)	April–Sept	Pink
Daisy	7.5cm (3in)	Feb–Nov	White
Heartsease	45cm (18in)	April–Sept	Yellow/purple
Navelwort	30cm (12in)	June–Aug	Yellow
Pasque Flower	30cm (12in)	March–May	Purple
Pimpernel – Scarlet	10cm (4in)	May–Aug	Red
Pineappleweed	30cm (12in)	May–Aug	Yellow
Pink – Maiden	45cm (18in)	June–Sept	Pink
Rockrose	30cm (12in)	May–Sept	Yellow
Saxifrage – Mossy	22cm (9in)	March–May	White
Scabious – Devil's Bit	60cm (24in)	July–Oct	Blue
Scurvy Grass	45cm (18in)	April–Sept	White
Silverweed	15cm (6in)	May–Sept	Yellow
Speedwell – Germander	20cm (8in)	April–July	Blue
Stonecrop – Biting	10cm (4in)	June–Aug	Yellow
Stonecrop – English	7.5cm (3in)	May–Aug	White
Strawberry – Wild	30cm (12in)	April–Sept	White
Thrift	30cm (12in)	May–Sept	Pink
Thyme – Wild	10cm (4in)	June–Sept	Mauve
Vervain	60cm (24in)	June–Sept	Mauve
Whitlow-grass – Yellow	10cm (4in)	March–Aug	Yellow

Chapter Three

Meadow Plants

MEADOW PLANTS

Althrough very few people have a garden big enough to accommodate a meadow, a small area of meadow plants can look very effective. Even a 1m by 3m (3ft by 9ft) brick-sided raised bed filled to overflowing with meadow plants can look quite spectacular and, contrary to popular belief, can be colourful far beyond the height of summer. The plants included here will provide colour from April right through the summer and autumn, the grasses and teasel giving interest and form through the winter as well.

Many meadow plants can be used in other situations as well. They are adapted to close planting and intense competition for water, light and nutrients, so will do equally well in a mixed border or the floor of an orchard. Mowing is no

MEADOW: THEMED RED

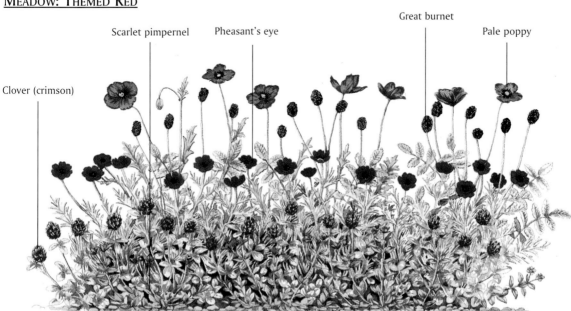

Clover (crimson) · Scarlet pimpernel · Pheasant's eye · Great burnet · Pale poppy

problem for many of them. Mature flowering heights are specified for the different plants, but many will flower at much shorter heights if they have been cut down early in the year. The usually 90cm (36in) mallows, for instance, will flower at just 10cm (4in) high at the edge of a lawn.

There are two basic types of meadows, populated by two different groups of plants. Wet meadows have plants that would be equally at home in a marshy area, whereas dry-meadow plants would be just as happy in a rockery. There is, of course, some overlap between the two groups. Also, early-mown or grazed meadows will often have a different flora from those mown later. The shorter grass areas could hold cowslips, orchids and bird's-foot trefoil, whereas the later-mown, longer grass might contain cornflowers, poppies, corn marigolds and cow parsley.

MEADOW: MAY & JUNE

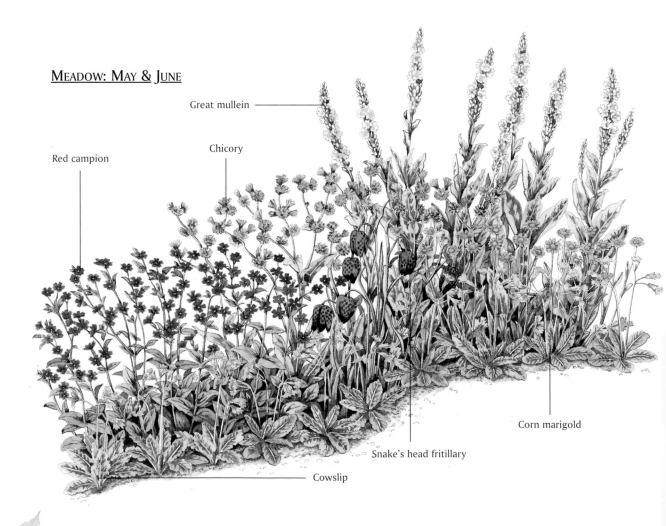

Great mullein

Chicory

Red campion

Corn marigold

Snake's head fritillary

Cowslip

Planting need not create a kaleidoscope of colours. A more limited palette can look equally effective. The pale pink of musk mallow, for example, combines very well with the rich yellow of ragwort or St John's Wort in a two-colour combination. In a red garden, poppies and knapweed, perhaps with sainfoin or red campion, look very good. Buttercups and ox-eye daisies make a lovely combination, or you can go for the multi-colour option and mix corn marigolds with annual cornflowers, poppies, ox-eye daisies and cow parsley for a summer extravaganza. The choice is yours, the seeds are available and you only need to buy them once, for although most of the meadow plants are annuals, they seed prolifically and should replace themselves with or without your help each year. If they are in the wrong place, all you need do is pull them up. If you are careful, then you can even replant them where you want them. Although wildflower meadows are rare now and becoming rarer with modern farm practices, they are still around in some places; once seen, they will truly inspire. There is nothing like the blaze of colour you can get in a good meadow to bring out the wish for such a brilliant display in your garden.

Meadow: Mixed with Grasses – June

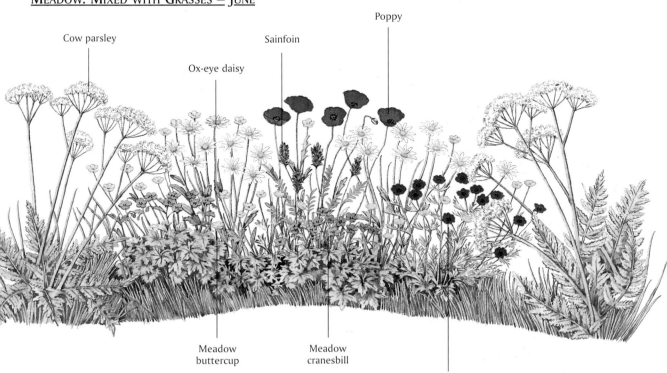

Cow parsley

Ox-eye daisy

Sainfoin

Poppy

Meadow buttercup

Meadow cranesbill

Pheasant's eye

Bedstraw – Lady's   *Galium verum*

This sweet-smelling perennial meadow flower was once dried and used to line mattresses. Its stems are up to 60cm (24in) tall but fairly weak and fine, needing the support of surrounding plants. Its long, dense panicles of bright-yellow flowers look excellent in combination with a number of – dare I say? – bedfellows. For an all-yellow effect, golden rod, mullein and wild parsnip make good companions, or for a mixed-colour arrangement red valerian, various bellflowers, cornflowers and poppies will make an attractive combination.

The bedstraws are a varied family, including the similar but taller and white-flowered hedge bedstraw (*G. mollugo*), sweet woodruff (*G. odoratum*), which is described in the chapter on shade flowers, and the much less welcome goose grass or cleavers *(G. aparine)*. This is that long, sticky (by means of tiny hooked hairs) plant with whorls of six to eight leaves along the stem, which leaves its tiny round seed pods on your clothes as you walk through meadows and grassy footpaths in late summer and autumn. Lady's bedstraw, however, has no such annoying habits. Its thickly clustered flowers are attractive to bees and will brighten a meadow garden or a mixed border, where it can be grown in close association with other plants from early June through to September.

Height: Up to 60cm (24in).

Habitat: Meadows, dry grassland and open woods, where it can find a sunny position.

Garden care: Dead-head to extend the flowering season. Best planted close to the house, so that the sweet scent can be enjoyed through the summer.

Propagation: Seed and plants are available from specialist nurseries throughout Britain. Seed should be sown in late summer or early autumn in pots or trays. Young plants can be planted out as soon as they are large enough to handle or kept in pots until springtime.

Buttercup
Ranunculus sp.

Several species of buttercup are native to Britain. Probably the most useful of these for the garden is the bulbous buttercup (*R. bulbosa*). This is the classic, golden-yellow, cup-shaped flower of childhood games. The flowers are about 2.5cm (1in) across with the sepals turned back along the furrowed stem. This plant enjoys drier conditions than the other buttercups and prefers lime-rich soil. Of its close relatives, the creeping buttercup (*R. repens*) is not recommended for garden use as it is too invasive. The leaves of this one are broader and the sepals stay tight to the backs of the petals. Another commonly found species is the meadow buttercup (*R. acris*). This is a much-branched plant, taller than the others at 1m (3ft), and its stems are not ridged like those of the others. The flower is cup-shaped, but the sepals lie close to the petals. The bulbous buttercup flowers in May and June, the others from May to September.

Height: Bulbous buttercup up to 40cm (16in).

Habitat: Bulbous buttercup prefers dry pasture, often lime rich. The others like moist soil.

Garden care: All species are plants of meadowland, so like a restricted root-run and some support. Plant close together for a bold statement or in close proximity to other plants for a more natural effect.

Propagation: Seeds are available from specialist wildflower nurseries.

Campion – Red
Silene dioica

This dioecious perennial – there are separate male and female plants – will thrive anywhere that it gets some shade for at least part of the day. The dark-pink flowers are about 2.5cm (1in) across and are borne on branching light-green stems up to 75cm (30in) high, rising from an evergreen rosette of oval hairy leaves. Leaves further up the stems are narrower, with shorter stalks. It begins to flower in April and continues well into the summer and intermittently through until late September. The petals are deeply notched at the tips and attractive to butterflies. The wild form is a very beautiful plant, but needs cutting down after flowering unless the seed is required. There is also a pretty double version with larger flowers called 'Flore Pleno', and a dwarf variety called 'Minnikin', which forms a neat hummock of downy leaves in a sunny spot and is liberally covered with pink flowers throughout the summer.

Height: 30–100cm (1–3ft).

Habitat: The shady side of hedgerows, ditches, woodlands and tall herb communities, usually on neutral to alkaline soils.

Garden care: Water in well when planting. Cut down flowering stems after flowering has finished unless seed is wanted.

Propagation: Seed and plants are available from nurseries, the cultivated forms as plants in some garden centres. Seed can be saved and sown in pots or where it is to flower, in autumn or spring. Plants can be divided every three years.

Campion – White   *Silene alba*

Having larger, fuller flowers than its close relative the red campion (*S. dioica*), the white campion is a plant of more open ground than its relative. It grows in the sunny edges of arable fields and on open waste ground, as well as close to the red campion in hedgerow bottoms, where the two occasionally hybridize to give a pale-pink offspring. The white campion flowers from May to October, its flowers a little over 2.5cm (1in) across and subtly scented, especially in the evening. It has male and female plants like the red campion and is taller than the bladder campion (*S. vulgaris*), for which it is occasionally confused at a distance. At closer quarters the lack of the inflated bladder-like calyx behind the flower is soon apparent.

Height: Up to 1m (3ft).

Habitat: Meadows, field margins, hedgerows and dry banks.

Garden care: Water in well when planting, which is best done in autumn or early spring. Dead-head to keep the flower display going through the season and cut the plants down to the basal rosette of stalked oval leaves in late autumn.

Propagation: Seed and plants are available from some nurseries. Seed should be sown in late summer or early autumn. Cuttings can be taken in summer and potted in plastic bags to root in a few weeks outside or in the cold frame.

Chamomile – Corn   *Anthemis arvensis*

A hairy plant with finely cut leaves, sometimes hairy underneath. It has neat daisy flowers 2–4cm (0.75–1.5in) across, borne in profusion over the plant from May to July and pleasantly, though not strongly, fragrant. Not to be confused with its close relative, also native, the stinking chamomile (*A. cotula*), which smells rank, is almost hairless and flowers from July to September. There is a third native chamomile: the lawn variety (*A. nobilis*), which is a perennial. This also has white daisy-type flowers, but is much stronger and sweeter smelling and flowers from June to August.

Height: 30–45cm (12–18in).

Habitat: Arable and wasteland. Prefers lime-rich soil and full sun.

Garden care: Dead-heading is important as without it there will be one good flush then no more.

Propagation: Lawn chamomile is widely available from nurseries and garden centres. Corn chamomile has to come from the more specialized places. Seed can be sown in autumn or spring, in trays or where it is to flower. Pruning the plants hard immediately after flowering, without allowing them to set seed, can sometimes make them last into the following year.

Cornflower – Annual *Centaurea cyanus*

This naturally blue-flowered annual has been through a lot of changes in the past forty years or so. Once common as a weed of arable land, it is now rare in the wild, but very common in gardens. It has been bred to give dwarf varieties as well as the full-sized ones and white, pink, or red-flowered types. Flowering from June to September, cornflowers give good value for money and the seeds are hardy, lasting for years if kept dry. A deservedly popular, slim grey-leaved plant for most types of garden.

Height: Up to 1m (3ft).

Habitat: Naturally a plant of dry grassland and arable fields, it can thrive in any well-drained soil, in sun or partial shade.

Garden care: Water in well when planting pot-grown plants. Dead-head regularly for a good, continuous show of flowers and pull out when flowering is finished.

Propagation: Seed is freely available from garden centres and nurseries. It can be sown in autumn or spring, as this is a hardy annual. Autumn-sown seed tends to give stronger, bushier plants. Seed can be saved from your own plants but will not necessarily be true to variety.

Cowslip *Primula veris*

This lovely spring flower is politely named for what it tends to grow best in – cow slop or dung. Its small yellow flowers with their long yellow green tubular calices behind nod gently in bunches at the tops of long, slender stems. The stems rise up from a basal rosette of crinkled, softly hairy, mid-green, tongue-like leaves. The flowers smell faintly of apricots. This plant has been crossed with its close relative, the primrose (*P. vulgaris*) to produce the multi-coloured primulas so readily available in spring from garden centres, market stalls and numerous other outlets. Its other close relative which is native to Britain is the oxlip (*P. elatior*), now a rare plant in the wild. This has larger, paler flowers with no scent and is a woodland flower, blooming from March to May. The cowslip flowers at the same time.

Height: Flowering stems up to 25cm (10in).

Habitat: Old grassland, including roadsides and orchards. Can tolerate sun or shade but is not a lover of excess moisture.

Garden care: Dead-head when the flowering stem has finished and the plant may well put up another and even another. A late one can be left on the plant if seed is required. Lift and divide clumps every couple of years.

Propagation: Plants and seed are available from nurseries and some garden centres. Seed needs to be sown fresh and will take until at least the next spring to germinate, as it needs the cold of winter to break its dormancy. Divide and replant clumps before flowering in spring.

Cranesbill – Meadow

Geranium pratense

One of a large group of plants, both native and foreign, several of which make good garden specimens. The meadow cranesbill enjoys the status of a widely used garden plant, its bright-blue flowers decorating the mixed border as well as its natural habitat from June to September, especially if it is regularly dead-headed. The dark-green leaves are deeply divided and sub-divided, normally in seven lobes coming from a central point where the stalk joins. The blue flowers are five-petalled cups about 2.5cm (1in) across, sometimes with black centres. They are held on branching stems above the leaves. There is an even more floriferous variety called 'Johnson's Blue' and a very handsome white one, predictably known as 'Alba'. The wood cranesbill (*G. sylvaticum*) also has blue flowers, though they are smaller and more mauve than the meadow cranesbill and the leaves are smaller and less divided. It flowers in June and July. Those particularly interested in geraniums will find whole books on the subject in many book shops and garden centres.

Height: Up to 60cm (24in), but more usually half that.

Habitat: Damp meadows, woodland and roadsides, in sun or light shade.

Garden care: Water in well when planting, dead-head regularly and tidy up old, dead leaves at the end of the growing season and you will be rewarded with a beautiful display for many years.

Propagation: Seed and plants are widely available from garden centres and nurseries. The wood cranesbill, along with some of the other less-used species, can be found in specialist nurseries. Mature plants can be dug up and divided in spring or autumn.

Hawk's-beard – Beaked

Crepis vesicaria

There are several species of hawk's-beard native to Britain. They are generally 60–100cm (2–3ft) tall and much branched, the yellow flowers resembling those of the dandelion and the hawkweeds. The beaked hawk's-beard is usually about 50cm (20in) tall, branched and wiry, its leaves slender and mostly at the base of the plant, divided like those of the dandelion. rough hawk's-beard (*C. biennis*) is taller, at about 1m (3ft), its flowers broader, but more ragged-looking, the buds shorter. smooth hawk's-beard (*C. capillaris*) is about the same height as beaked hawk's-beard, but the flowers are a darker yellow and the buds more rounded. Like rough hawk's-beard, it grows throughout the British Isles, being common in grassland, waste ground and roadsides, flowering in late summer and autumn. Smooth hawk's-beard is the one that may be found on walls and dry slopes. There is also a marsh hawk's-beard, whose flowers are covered with black hairs and which is found in high marshes and bogs in Wales and Scotland. Of them all beaked hawk's-beard is the earliest into flower, blooming in May and continuing all the way through the summer.

Height: Up to 60cm (24in).

Habitat: Meadows and grassland, especially on lime-rich soils.

Garden care: Best sown where it is to flower so that it can establish its crown tight against the soil, this plant will then not need any support. Otherwise the wiry stems will fall over if not grown in close association with other plants. Dead-head regularly to keep the strength in the plant, leaving a few heads on if seed is required towards the end of the flowering season.

Propagation: Seed is available from specialist wildflower nurseries. Sow where it is required to flower in autumn or early spring and water in well.

Below: Smooth hawk's-beard.

Knapweed – Common

Centaurea nigra

A hairy plant with elliptical leaves all the way up the stem. The flower head is quite tight and thistle-like, the bud hard and scaled with dark-brown bracts. Closely related is the greater knapweed (*C. scabiosa*) which is slightly taller, has large divided basal leaves and small, narrowstem-leaves. The flowers are larger, more open and ragged-looking, with long inflorescences around the outside of the head. Both of these flower between June and September.

Height: Common knapweed grows up to 60cm (24in), greater knapweed up to about 1m (3ft).

Habitat: Both are found in meadows, grassland and on footpaths. Common knapweed is sometimes seen on cliffs.

Garden care: These plants like plenty of sun and can take a dryish soil, but need a deep root-run. Although they are meadow plants, they are generally able to support themselves without staking.

Propagation: Seed and plants can be found in most garden centres.

Marigold – Corn *Chrysanthemum segetum*

Bright-yellow, daisy-like flowers up to 5cm (2in) across make a bold statement in a summer meadow or border. This upright, branching annual flowers from June to September above smooth, scented, bluish-green, fleshy leaves. A plant that looks spectacular in a bold group.

Height: 15–45cm (6–18in), depending on the closeness of planting.

Habitat: Once a common weed of cornfields, it is now a rare denizen of sunny, preferably sandy, arable land and waste ground, where its seed can lie dormant for several years if undisturbed.

Garden care: Provide a site with plenty of sun. A light soil is preferred but not essential. Dead-head regularly until you want to harvest seed towards the end of the flowering season. Cutting back hard before the plant sets seed may make it last another year.

Propagation: Seed is available from specialist nurseries and easy to collect from your own plants.

Mullein – Great *Verbascum thapsus*

Another native plant that has found a home in our gardens, the great mullein or common mullein grows as a biennial, having a large rosette of grey, felty leaves in the first year. From these arise tall, usually unbranched flowering stems in the late spring of the second year. These stems have leaves up their lower portions, leading up to a flower spike that can be 1m (3ft) long and dotted seemingly at random with open yellow flowers about 2.5cm (1in) across. The whole plant is covered in a thick silver down and is one of those plants that is designed to make a bold statement in the garden. The multi-coloured garden cultivars of *Verbascum* sold in garden centres are bred from two other species, the purple mullein (*V. phoeniceum*), which is not native, and the dark mullein (*V. nigrum*), which is native and is a handsome plant in its own right. Dark mullein grows to anything up to 1.2m (4ft) high, with dark stems and dark centres to the yellow flowers but lacking the thick hairs of great mullein.

Height: Up to 2.1m (7ft).

Habitat: Woodland clearings, roadsides, dry banks and scrub. Tolerates chalk and sandy soils well. Can take partial shade. Flowers best in dry soil with a poor nutrient content.

Garden care: Plant in poor soil for best results and cut down the flowering stem as soon as it has finished flowering in order to keep the plant for another year.

Propagation: Available from nurseries and garden centres. Plants will self-seed if allowed to do so. Root cuttings can be taken before planting out in spring and rooted in pots.

Ox-eye Daisy

Leucanthemum vulgare

Sometimes also listed as *Chrysanthemum leucanthemum*, this branched, woody-based perennial is also commonly known as the moon daisy. They are very variable in height, depending on where they are growing, but commonly provide sheets of white on roadsides, dry banks and meadows from late May well into August. The large, daisy-like flowers open at the tops of sparsely hairy green stems with leaves similar to those of the garden chrysanthemums. The basal leaves are long-stalked and rounded, the stem leaves unstalked, long and slender, both with coarsely toothed margins. Ox-eye daisies are well worth growing in a sunny spot in the garden.

Height: 10–60cm (4–24in), depending on density of planting, how sunny the site is and how moist.

Habitat: Naturally found in grassland, on dry banks and railway edges as well as open woodland. Prefers neutral to alkaline soils.

Garden care: Water pot-grown plants in well when planting. Dead-head regularly to keep flowering at its best through the season and cut back hard in autumn, after flowering has finished. Mulch with organic matter in spring and divide clumps every three years.

Propagation: Plants and seed are available from nurseries. Cuttings can be taken in spring, also plants can be lifted and divided at this time of year.

Parsnip – Wild

Pastinaca sativa

This perennial herb, resembling cow parsley (*Anthriscus sylvestris*) and its relatives, but with yellow flowers, has a strong tap-root: this was bred to become thicker and more fleshy until it became the parsnip that is grown as a vegetable in our gardens today. The stiff, downy stems arise in early summer, pale and thick, with rough pinnate leaves folding out from them, their broad lobes toothed. The upper leaves are often very small. The hollow, ridged stems are branched and darken with age to a rich green colour. The tiny bright-yellow flowers are borne in much-branched flat terminal panicles from July to September. The plant can provide a stately contrast to the verticals of golden rod (*Solidago virgaurea*), yellow loosestrife (*Lysimachia vulgaris*) or purple loosestrife (*Lythrum salicaria*), for instance, in the middle or back of a mixed border.

Height: Up to 1.2m (4ft).

Habitat: Grassy slopes, meadows, roadsides and ditches, especially on chalk and limestone soils.

Garden care: Ultra-violet light can sometimes react with chemicals in the plant to make it irritating to the skin, so gloves are best worn when handling it, just in case. The plant should be watered in well when planting, preferably in a deep soil, and not allowed to dry out too much through the growing season of the first year. Cutting off the flower heads when they are finished may encourage the production of more heads, extending the flowering season into October. The plant can be cut down to ground level in late autumn.

Propagation: Seed is available from some nurseries and should be sown in mid to late summer in pots or where it is to flower. Pot-grown plants can be planted out in late spring or early summer. Seed can be saved from existing plants by enclosing the flower head in a paper bag once it has finished flowering and tying the bag tight, then bending the head downwards.

Pheasant's Eye

Adonis annua

This feathery-leaved annual is a member of the buttercup family, along with the spearworts and, less obviously, the meadow rues *thalictrum* species. It bears 4cm (1.5in) wide, cup-shaped red flowers with black centres from May to August, reminiscent of a small cosmos. This is a deservedly popular garden plant with big, starry, daisy-like flowers, growing to about 75cm (30in). The pheasant's eye flowers are borne singly at the tips of the branched stems. The finely cut pinnate leaves are stalkless, providing a smoky haze of bright green as a background to the vivid flowers. There are four species of pheasant's eye, but only two occur in Britain, the second being large pheasant's eye (*A. flammea*), which is very similar, but has a softly hairy stem. The other two are both European plants: summer pheasant's eye (*A. aestivalis*) has longer, paler petals with definite black bases and spring pheasant's eye is a perennial with large, bright-yellow flowers.

Height: Up to 30cm (12in).

Habitat: Open grassland and arable land in southern England.

Garden care: Best sown where it is to flower. Rake the soil lightly after sowing and water, then simply keep weed-free and dead-head as necessary.

Propagation: Seed and plants are available from specialist nurseries. Seed can be saved from existing plants, but like other members of the buttercup family it is best sown fresh.

Poppy – Common

Papaver rhoeas

One of only two truly red flowers native to Britain, the other being the pheasant's eye (*Adonis annua*), the common poppy makes a glorious sight when massed in summer meadows or on roadsides. There are four distinct species of poppy which can be defined by close examination. The others include the long-headed poppy (*P. dubium*), similar to the common poppy, but with long, narrow fruits (this is sometimes found in a very attractive orange form, as well as the usual red). The rough poppy (*P. hybridum*), has a hairy fruit, rounded like that of the common poppy; the prickly poppy (*P. argemone*) has a fruit similar in shape to that of the long-headed poppy but hairy, and the petals are smaller, narrower and well separated. Having said all that, the common poppy gives a wonderful show from May to September, the papery flowers displayed above bristly bright-green stems and divided, hairy leaves, and the bristly buds nodding gently between the open flowers with their deep-black centres.

Height: 20–45cm (8–18in), depending on the density of surrounding planting.

Habitat: Cornfields, waste ground, footpaths and roadside verges, especially where the ground has been disturbed – which has to be a good reason for using a hoe between your plants.

Garden care: Frequent dead-heading through the summer will ensure a long display of flowers. Leave a few heads to ripen towards the end of the flowering season and hoe between the plants to encourage seed to set.

Propagation: Seed is available from nurseries or once you have the plants you can save your own, though it is best sown fresh, where it is to flower.

Queen Anne's Lace   *Anthriscus sylvestris*

Also known as cow parsley and keck in different parts of the country, this plant is one of literally dozens that are native to Britain among the parsley family. Many of them are useful in the garden. Several are edible and have parented cultivated vegetables and herbs. Others, like hemlock (*Conium maculatum*), are poisonous. The difficulty comes in telling some of them apart. Queen Anne's lace is, however, a useful species in the garden purely for decorative reasons. Its fine filigree of dark-green leaves beneath delicate white sprays of tiny flowers make an excellent substitute for gypsophilla, both in the border and in the vase. It flowers from April to August, repeatedly if dead-headed regularly, and its height will vary according to its growing conditions – how dense the planting is and how much sun it gets.

Height: Can grow to 1.5cm (5ft), but commonly settles for half that, especially in full sun.

Habitat: Roadsides, meadows, scrub and woodland. It will grow in sun or shade, in dry or damp soils.

Garden care: Water in well when planting, but this should not be needed thereafter. Dead-head regularly to improve flowering.

Allow a few heads to stay on at the end of the season and set seed for collection. Leave the old plants in the border over winter, as the dry skeletons look very decorative in a winter frost.

Propagation: Seed is available from specialist nurseries or can be saved from existing plants and sown in pots outside or where the plants are required, preferably in autumn.

Ragwort – Common   *Senecio jacobaea*

This plant, which is poisonous to cattle and horses, is one of four native ragworts. They are the British representatives, along with groundsel, of a genus which has a truly worldwide distribution and includes annuals, herbaceous perennials, shrubs and succulents. Common ragwort is the largest of the native species, standing up to 1m (3ft) tall, with lobed leaves and umbel-like groups of thin-petalled daisy flowers at the branched top of the plant from June to September. Oxford ragwort (*S. squalidus*) is half the height, more branched, its leaves much more finely divided with the upper ones tending to clasp the stems and its flowers, up to 2.5cm (1in)

across, having wider, fuller petals. It flowers from June right through to December. The marsh ragwort (*S. aquaticus*) is a darker plant, the leaves much less divided – lower leaves often entire – which grows to about 75cm (30in) tall. Its flowers are up to 4cm (1.5in) across and much less bunched than the other species, the width of the petals between those of the common and Oxford ragworts. This one flowers through July and August. The fourth native species is the hoary ragwort (*S. crucifolius*). This is very similar to the common ragwort, differing slightly in the structure of the flowers.

Height: Common: up to 1m (3ft). Marsh: up to 85cm (34in). Oxford: up to 45cm (18in).

Habitat: Common: dry grassland and tall herb communities. Marsh: marshes, ditches and wet meadows. Oxford: walls, waste ground, path edges.

Garden care: A sunny position in almost any garden soil will keep these plants happy, though obviously the marsh ragwort needs plenty of moisture. If stressed, they may suffer from powdery

mildew or the tomato-spotted wilt virus, but otherwise are trouble free. Thorough dead-heading is recommended, both to prolong flowering and to prevent excessive spreading. Also, the plants are kept in control by lifting and dividing every two or three years in spring. Cut the plants down to ground level in December.

Propagation: By division every two or three years in April or May, or by seed, which can be sown where it is to grow in autumn or into seed trays of a heavyish compost.

Restharrow – Common

Ononis repens

Obtaining its name by binding – or arresting – the harrow in old meadowland, this tough-stemmed perennial of the pea family bears showy, pink, pea-like flowers from July until the autumn, though sadly they are without scent. It is most commonly found on dry grassland, but will take well to rockeries or walls. This is one of the non-climbing members of the genus, though it will form a tough tangle of stems, well endowed with flowers through the late summer. Its close relative spiny restharrow (*O. spinosa*) is a little taller at 45cm (18in), its flowers are redder and it prefers heavier soils (the other difference, of course, being its spiny nature).

Height: 30cm (12in).

Habitat: Both plants are usually found in dry grassland, path edges and waste ground. They grow in most soil types.

Garden care: Plenty of sunlight is important to these plants. They will be happy in the border or the rockery, but do not allow them to be swamped by their neighbours and they will reward you with a long show of colour.

Propagation: Like sweet peas, seed can be sown in autumn or spring. Opinion is divided as to the benefits of either option, but the seed needs to be scarified before sowing. Seed is available from specialist wildflower nurseries.

Sainfoin

Onobrychis viciifolia

Retaining its French name (which means 'wholesome hay') from the time of the Normans, this stiffly erect perennial member of the pea family has long been grown as a fodder crop throughout many parts of Europe, including England. The pinnate leaves are about 10cm (4in) long and divided into many elliptical leaflets with hairs on the undersides. The robust stems are branching, the plant forming a small bush-like growth, topped with a profusion of round arrow-head-shaped racemes of dark-pink flowers from May to August, each flower spike being about 5cm (2in) long.

Height: Up to 60cm (24in).

Habitat: Field edges, roadsides and dry banks, often on limestone or chalk soils.

Garden care: Water in well when planting in spring until it is established, but then only if the soil really dries out in the next few weeks. Dead-head regularly to prolong the flowering period and cut back hard at the end of the growing season.

Propagation: Seed and plants are available from specialist nurseries. Seed can be saved from existing plants. Cuttings can be taken in summer and rooted in pots of sharp compost, sealed into plastic bags.

Scabious – Field

Knautia arvensis

Reaching up to 1m (3ft) tall, this is the largest of the native scabious species. Its lilac-blue flowers are up to 5cm (2in) across, though they lack the papery outer ring of petals of the garden varieties, which are bred from an eastern European species. Its hairy stems are surprisingly strong, and the stem leaves finely cut, though the basal ones are slender, undivided but toothed. All leaves are stalkless. With larger, paler flowers than the devil's bit scabious mentioned elsewhere, the field scabious is of similar maximum height and flowering season – from July until the first frosts – and also likes as much sun as its can get. Naturally a meadow plant, it makes a very good specimen for the middle to rear of a border, where it can be combined with a range of other species to good effect, attracting the attentions of a steady stream of bees. Small scabious (*S. columbaria*) is a similar species 30cm (12in) tall, with pale-blue flowers.

Height: Up to 1m (3ft).

Habitat: Meadows and grassland, including roadsides and dry slopes.

Garden care: Can tolerate most soils, though acid-free is preferable. Slugs can damage new growth in spring, so a few pellets or a grit mulch can be useful. Dead-heading will keep the plants tidy, though it makes little difference to the length of the flowering season. Plants can be cut down after flowering has finished in autumn.

Propagation: Seed and plants are available from specialist nurseries. Seed can be saved from established plants. Clumps can be dug up and divided in spring.

Teasel

Dipsacus fullonum

This stately biennial, much loved of flower arrangers down the ages, is also very useful in the woollen industry, for which it is still specifically grown in Somerset. This is for the rough, hooked bracts that are used to raise the nap on newly woven cloth. In its first year, the teasel forms a rosette of prostrate prickly leaves up to 30cm (12in) long while its thick tap root runs long and deep into the earth. It is in the second year that the tall, branched stem rises up, angular, spiny and pale green in colour. The stem leaves are long and pointed, with spines on their undersides and often toothed edges, growing in opposite pairs from the stem. The oval flower heads are surrounded at their bases by small leaves and the pink flowers open in rings around the head, attracting bees and butterflies in profusion. Then the plant sets seed and dies, but the skeletal brown form remains over winter and often through the next year, providing a vital source of seeds to small finches through the cold months. Teasels flower in July and August and are ideal for the edge of a meadow garden or the middle of a mixed border, adding structure in a striking fashion from June onwards.

Height: Up to 1.8m (6ft).

Habitat: Waste ground, pastures and river banks. Can take wet or dry soil, but likes sun.

Garden care: Take care to wear gloves when handling this plant, as it is spiny just about all over, but very little handling should be needed until it is time to tidy up the old, dead plants the year after flowering.

Propagation: From seed, which is available from nurseries or can be saved from existing plants. Best sown where it is to flower, as the strong root system is not suited to growing in pots or trays. As for other biennials, sow in mid to late summer.

Vetch – Common

Vicia sativa

This weak-stemmed annual will sprawl over the ground or climb through other plants by means of the usual twining tendrils at the tips of the leaf stalks. The leaves are pinnate: the leaflets in three to eight pairs may be narrow and linear or oval, about 2cm (0.75in) long. The pea-like pink flowers are borne singly or in pairs in the axils of the upper leaves. They are up to 2cm (0.75in) across. The plant was widely grown as a fodder crop in the past, but makes an interesting addition to a raised bed or rockery, where the flowers can be appreciated close-up during the full length of the summer from mid-May to September.

Height: Up to 50cm (20in).

Habitat: Grassland and footpath edges. Enjoys full sun.

Garden care: Give the plant a sunny position and perhaps a spring-flowering plant for it to twine up or over. Dead-head regularly to extend the flowering period, like all members of the pea family.

Propagation: Towards the end of the flowering season, allow a few pods to form and ripen. They are like small pea pods and go black when ripe. Collect the seed and sow when fresh. If you have to store the seed or buy it from a nursery, then a light scarification with fine sand-paper before sowing will aid germination. Seed is available from wild flower nurseries.

Yarrow

Achillea millefolium

There are numerous yarrows sold in garden centres and nurseries for the garden, with vivid colours through the range of yellows, oranges and reds as well as pinks and white. Most of these are not varieties of the native yarrow, but bred from two of the foreign species. However, there is a variety called 'Cerise Queen' which bears oval heads of deep-pink flowers and does originate from the native species. Our own yarrow usually has white flowers, though there are occasional pink and purple sports in the wild. The flowers form tight, branched heads very like those of the parsley and carrot families, but smaller and denser. These are held at the tops of the little-branched, furrowed and woolly stems with their small, feathery leaves from June to October. The plant is a perennial, the stems rising up from creeping ground stems each spring. The subtle white heads contrast well with more stridently coloured flowers in summer, such as purple loosestrife (*Lythrum salicaria*) or some of the bellflowers.

Height: Up to 50cm (20in).

Habitat: Meadows, woodland clearings, roadsides and dry grassland. Prefers full sun.

Garden care: If you want the plant to grow in an exposed, open site, then it is best grown from seed where it is required. Otherwise it will need staking. However, in a more sheltered position or in a meadow environment with the support of other plants this will not be necessary. Yarrow can withstand dry conditions. It should be cut down to just above ground level once flowering has finished.

Propagation: Seed and plants of the native yarrow are available from nurseries. Occasionally, the coloured varieties of this plant are seen in garden centres with the more usual cultivated ones of foreign origin. The plants can be dug up and divided every three years, basal cuttings can be taken in spring or seed can be saved and sown in spring, where it is to flower.

GRASSES

Apart from their obvious use in the lawn, grasses are highly decorative plants for a number of situations in the garden, adding their particular form and texture to beds and borders, in sun or shade as well as in the marshy places or even in the pond. There are three types of plants growing wild in Britain with long, narrow stems and leaves and wind-born pollen which are, or can be mistaken for, grasses. The sedges are usually plants of wetland habitat. Most have several groups of flowers along the stem, which is triangular in section, the leaves having a strong mid-rib on their underside. The rushes have tubular stems, often with a pithy centre, and the leaves tend to be rolled lengthwise so that they are round in section and there is no upper or lower surface. The true grasses have jointed stems, often with a leaf arising from the joint. The stems are round and the leaves usually flat, the base of the leaf often wrapped around the stem from where it emerges. So too are those of the reeds, which are simply large grasses, usually of wetland habitats. There are over 17,000 species of grasses, sedges and reeds worldwide. Many species have potential as attractive border or meadow plants.

Meadow Grass – Wood *Poa nemoralis*

A loosely tufted perennial, this common grass is tolerant of sun or shade, growing in parks and meadows as well as the woods from which it draws its name. It is a hairless plant with thin, pale-green leaves and a loose, finely branched flower spike that is somewhat nodding until flowering is over, when it becomes erect. A very pretty and adaptable little grass, usually growing to about 30cm (12in) high, though it can be considerably taller in a shady situation. It dies back in winter, when the tufts can be cut short in preparation for next year's growth.

Dog's-tail – Crested *Cymosurus cristatus*

Tufted perennial up to 75cm (30in) tall with erect, smooth stalks and leaves that sometimes curl lengthwise. Flower panicles are dense, spike-like and greenish, with the spikelets arranged in two rows up the stem. These are quite one-sided, the stem itself angling in a wavy fashion from one pair of spikelets to the next and back again. Crested dog's-tail flowers in June and July, growing naturally in meadows and on the sides of roads and paths, generally in sunny situations. The plant persists long into the autumn, when it is more noticeable in the wild, for it is too tough to be grazed by animals.

Feather Grass – Common

Stipa pennata

Although seen in the photograph growing next to a pool near Oxford, England on the kind of dry, grassy, sunny bank it likes, feather grass was actually introduced from Europe because of its highly decorative appearance. It is a perennial, growing to a little over 60cm (24in) tall. The bristly leaves are a greyish green in colour, the heads and hairs on them silvery in the sunshine. Shown here in May, just before the true inflorescences appear, when they emerge they will be long and feathery, waving and curling in the breeze. This grass is rare in the wild in Britain but very worthwhile in the garden. It can be found in nurseries and some garden centres.

Wild Oat – Common   *Avena fatua*

The loose, drooping panicles of flower and later seed of this useful annual nod in the breeze from April onwards, drying on the stem if left, to give a golden haze to the border in winter and readily seed itself for the following year. The jointed, grass-like stems grow up to 60cm (24in). These and the rough leaves are a light-green colour. The long, narrow flowers hang from the tips of fine, branching stems. Very elegant when grown with something dark behind or through something shorter and rounded in form, such as the perennial cornflower (*Centaurea montana*) or some of the campanulas. A plant of sunny places on roadsides and waste ground, it needs some moisture, so is best watered in very dry weather.

Quaking Grass

Briza media

This perennial grass forms loose tufts of mid-green leaves up to about 15cm (6in) high. From these, in May and through to August, arise tall, very slender flowering stems, pale green turning to straw colour. The stems bear loose, very open panicles of flowers. These are born in heart-shaped bunches, each about 0.5cm (0.2in) across. These bunches, or spikelets,

of flowers are borne widely separated on long, branching stalks and begin life a pale-purple colour, with the yellow stamens hanging prominently. The stalks are so fine that the heads wave constantly in the slightest breeze, giving the grass its common name. Very decorative on a rockery or somewhere with a dark background.

Height: Up to 60cm (24in).

Habitat: Hedgerows and grassland, mainly on chalk or limestone, in sun or partial shade.

Garden care: Water in well when planting and until established, and lift and divide clumps every three years or so. Clip as required. The plant's leaves are generally quite tough and resistant to

infection, but if a rust disease does take hold, then use a proprietary fungicide.

Propagation: Plants and seed are available from some nurseries. Clumps can be lifted and divided every three years. Seed can be harvested and sown into pots or trays outside, or where the plant is to flower in late summer or autumn.

MEADOW PLANTS

	HEIGHT	FLOWERING SEASON	FLOWER COLOUR
Lady's Bedstraw	60cm (24in)	June–Sept	Yellow
Buttercups	40cm (16in)	May–Sept	Yellow
Campion – Red	1m (3ft)	April–Sept	Pink
Campion – White	1m (3ft)	May–Oct	White
Chamomile – Corn	45cm (18in)	May–July	White
Cornflower – Annual	1m (3ft)	June–Sept	Blue
Cowslip	25cm (10in)	March–May	Yellow
Cranesbill – Meadow	60cm (24in)	June–Sept	Blue
Hawk's-beard – Beaked	60cm (24in)	May–Aug	Yellow
Knapweed – Common	60cm (24in)	June–Sept	Purple
Marigold – Corn	45cm (18in)	June–Sept	Yellow
Mullein – Great	2.1m (7ft)	June–Aug	Yellow
Ox-eye Daisy	60cm (24in)	May–Aug	White
Parsnip – Wild	1.2m (4ft)	July–Sept	Yellow
Pheasant's Eye	1m (3ft)	May–Aug	Red
Poppy – Common	45cm (18in)	May–Sept	Red
Queen Anne's Lace	1.5m (5ft)	April–Aug	White
Ragwort – Common	1m (3ft)	June–Sept	Yellow
Restharrow – Common	30cm (12in)	July–Oct	Pink
Sainfoin	60cm (24in)	May–Aug	Pink
Scabious – Field	1m (3ft)	July–Oct	Blue
Teasel	1.8m (6ft)	July–Aug	Pink
Vetch – Common	50cm (20in)	May–Sept	Pink
Yarrow	50cm (20in)	June–Oct	White

Chapter Four

Marsh and Bog Plants

Marsh and Bog Plants

There are so many beautiful wetland plants that it would be a shame not to include at least some of them in any garden. Some will grow in drier conditions as well as in wet soil, such as the yellow loosestrife (*Lysimachia vulgaris*) and its low-growing cousin creeping jenny (*L. nummularia*), as well as the willowherbs and meadowsweet (*Filipendula ulmaria*). These, then, can be used to merge the wetland area into the rest of the garden. Others, though, are more strict in their requirements and with these, the soil conditions in which they grow naturally must be considered when choosing plants for your garden. Some plants are specifically adapted to the acid soils of peat bogs and sphagnum marshes, in the same way as the rhododendrons and camellias from Asia. Others can tolerate these conditions but are just as happy in neutral soils, and still others dislike acid soil entirely.

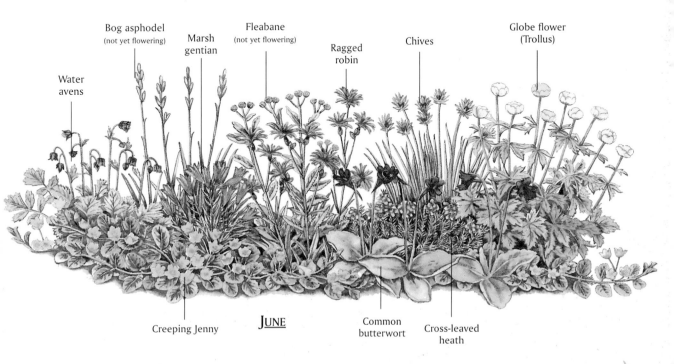

Water avens

Bog asphodel
(not yet flowering)

Marsh gentian

Fleabane
(not yet flowering)

Ragged robin

Chives

Globe flower
(Trollus)

Creeping Jenny

JUNE

Common butterwort

Cross-leaved heath

Before humans started draining bogs and marshes for agriculture and for building land such habitats covered large areas of Britain, but now only a fraction of that is left in isolated pockets, mainly in Scotland, Wales and northern and eastern England. Areas such as Tregaron Bog in West Wales, Wicken Fen in Cambridgeshire and the Norfolk Broads can be visited to see marsh and wetland plants in their natural habitat in safety. There are many other spots throughout Britain, some owned and managed by such organizations as local wildlife trusts, the National Trust and others. These will all be arranged to allow safe access. They are well worth visiting, especially during early to mid summer, when the butterflies abound and the flowers are at their best. Not that this is the only time of year when wetland plants provide interest and colour. Far from it, for the earliest begin to flower in March and several will continue into September or beyond. Then, through autumn and winter, interest is maintained by the evergreen rushes; the grasses which, though now only dead stems, remain upright; and the shrubs that enjoy this type of environment, such as cross-leaved heath (*Erica tetralix*), cranberry (*Vaccinium oxycoccos*) and bog myrtle or sweet gale (*Myrica gale*), among others.

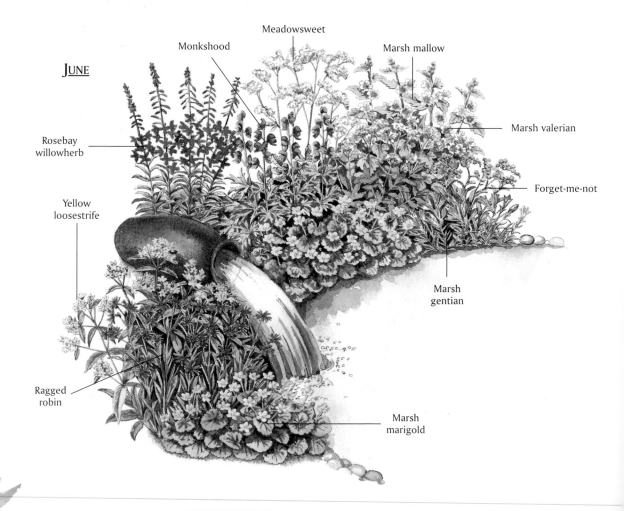

JUNE

Monkshood

Meadowsweet

Marsh mallow

Marsh valerian

Rosebay willowherb

Forget-me-not

Yellow loosestrife

Marsh gentian

Ragged robin

Marsh marigold

This is also the environment of some of Britain's stranger natives, such as the round-leaved sundew (*Drosera rotundifolia*) and its relatives, as well as some of the most beautiful, among them the orchids. And who could have a garden and not want to include the lovely yellow flag (*Iris pseudacorus*) or the globe flower (*Trollius europaeus*)?

Some may use the excuse that a bog garden is not easy to create in a garden where there is not a natural place for it, and it has to be said that it is easier to work with your conditions than against them. Still, a bog garden is no more difficult than a pond to set up – easier, in fact, for you do not have to make sure that the liner will not get holes in. Indeed, it needs some holes for drainage, for the soil in it needs to be wet, not stagnant. The bog garden can be linked to a pond or be an independent feature. It needs digging out to about 45cm (18in) deep, then lining with a polythene liner or something similar with several holes punched in it, then filling in again with soil, mixed with ericaceous compost if you want to include some of the acid bog species. Soak well using the hosepipe before planting. A mulch with bark chippings or cut reeds will help to retain moisture by preventing evaporation until the plants have established and filled out, then a check needs to be kept on the soil to make sure it does not dry out. Now plants like ferns, willowherbs, fleabane (*Pulicaria dysenterica*) and ragged robin (*Lychnis flos-cuculi*) can be enjoyed in all their lush glory.

AUGUST

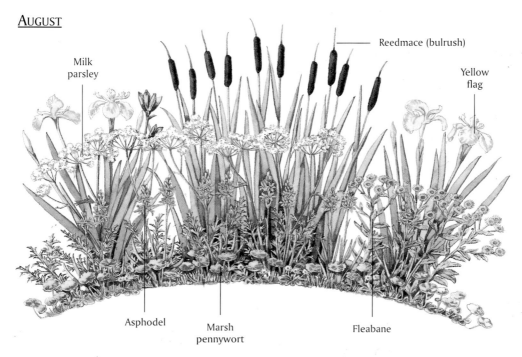

Milk parsley

Reedmace (bulrush)

Yellow flag

Asphodel

Marsh pennywort

Fleabane

Avens – Water

Geum rivale

Red flowers droop at the heads of erect stems, themselves a reddish colour, from May through to August. The basal leaves are large, rough and divided into broad lobes with serrated edges. They are soft and hairy and dull green in colour. Further up the stems, a few leaves are seen, much smaller and finer, divided into three segments and often a lighter green. This medium-sized perennial flowers copiously, the flowering stems much-branched and bent by the weight of the 2cm (0.75in) wide, bell-shaped flower. They straighten again when the fruits form into burr-like, spiny mid-brown spheres. Closely related to the geums of garden border use, with their bright red or yellow double flowers, there are also two other native species: the wood avens (*G. urbanum*), which is a common weed of gardens and waste ground with small yellow flowers at the tops of sparse, upright stems from May to August; and mountain avens (*Dryas octopetala*), which is a small, attractive plant with eight-petalled white flowers from June to August, growing in highland areas of northern Britain.

Height: Up to 1m (3ft), but commonly half that.

Habitat: Stream-sides, marshes and damp woods, mostly in northern Britain. Water Avens can tolerate sun or shade and any soil type, as long as it is water-retentive. Grows well in the herbaceous border on clay soils, but needs watering if the soil dries out.

Garden care: Water in well when planting and if the soil dries out thereafter. Dead-head regularly to extend the flowering period and cut back the flowering stems in autumn.

Propagation: Seed and plants are available from some garden centres and nurseries. Plants grow from an underground rhizome and can be divided in spring or autumn. Seed can be sown in spring to flower the same year, or in summer to flower next year. Sow in pots or trays or where the plants are required.

Bedstraw – Marsh *Galium palustre*

There are a dozen different species of bedstraw native to the British Isles, of which the most commonly known are lady's bedstraw (*G. verum*), described in the chapter on meadow plants; hedge bedstraw (*G. mollugo*), which is very similar to the marsh bedstraw; and goose grass or cleavers (*G. aparine*), that sticky, trailing weed which leaves little bristly balls attached to your clothes when you walk past it in late summer or autumn. The marsh bedstraw has small white flowers throughout the summer months. Like the other species, the flowers have four petals and the leaves are borne in whorls around the slender stems. Although the stems are weak, marsh bedstraw is more upright than either the small wood bedstraw or the trailing heath bedstraw. It clambers among more rigid plants, leaning on them for support and providing colour after many of its supporters have finished flowering. Looks very good growing with purple loosestrife (*Lythrum salicaria*) or marsh woundwort (*Stachys palustris*).

Height: Up to 60cm (2ft).

Habitat: Marshes, bogs and pond margins, often among reeds and rushes.

Garden care: Best grown in close combination with other tall plants, such as rushes etc. Cut back to half height after flowering has finished and to the base of the stems in late autumn.

Propagation: Plants and seed are available from specialist nurseries. Seed can be saved from existing plants and sown in damp compost in late summer.

Bird's-foot Trefoil – Greater

Lotus uliginosus

Looking like a large, often hairy version of the common bird's-foot trefoil described in the chapter on rockery plants, this perennial of the pea family has rather bluish-green leaves divided into three oval leaflets. The leaves are few for the size of the plant, which has long, hollow stems. The flowers, about 1cm (0.5in) long or a little more, are rich yellow and carried in round heads of eight or more from June through August. Each head is at the tip of a slender stalk up to 15cm (6in) long. Very decorative among rushes or reeds.

Height: Up to 75cm (30in).

Habitat: Marshes, fens and damp meadows.

Garden care: Dead-head regularly to extend flowering season, cut back to ground level at the end of autumn and feed with organic fertilizer in spring.

Propagation: Plants and seed are available from a few specialist nurseries. Seed can be saved from existing plants in the garden and sown in pots of damp compost in late summer or early autumn. Seed should be sown fresh or scarified before sowing – that is, the seed coat should be scratched to aid germination.

Bog Asphodel

Narthecium ossifragum

The light-green, sword-shaped leaves of this member of the lily family are arranged in two rows on the stems, becoming ever smaller as they near the flower spike. Once used in Lancashire as a hair dye, it is commonest in the north and west of Britain, on upland bogs. It bears short spikes of star-like yellow flowers which mature to a light orange from early July well into August. Well worth seeking out if you have a suitable home for it.

Height: Up to 30cm (12in).

Habitat: Acid bogs and peaty marshes. Needs acid conditions and full sun.

Garden care: Ensure conditions are suitable before planting. Dead-head unless the seed are required and cut the leaves down at the end of autumn.

Propagation: Plants are available from specialist nurseries and some water garden centres. Seed can be saved and sown in damp compost outside in late summer. Plants can be lifted and divided in spring or autumn, every three years or so.

Butterbur

Petasites hybridus

The rhubarb-like leaves of this sturdy perennial can be seen commonly in damp places throughout England and Wales. The broad, palmate, mid-green leaves can be up to 1m (3ft) across, on thick, coarsely hairy stems which begin to grow at about the time when the flowers are open, in spring. Popular with bees, the flowers of both male and female plants are pinkish, without petals, each about 0.7cm (0.3in) across and borne in spikes up to 60cm (24in) tall. The female spike is a lot looser and less dense than the male, which is shorter and more rounded. Very similar to the huge, imported gunnera, but a fraction of the size.

Height: Up to about 1m (3ft).

Habitat: Stream and ditch margins, marshes and wet meadows. Can thrive in sun or shade.

Garden care: Unlike the larger gunnera, this plant is fully hardy. The leaves can be cut off to the base at the end of the season for the sake of neatness and the flower stems can be cut back after flowering has finished, about May.

Propagation: Plants and seed are available from some specialist nurseries. Clumps can be lifted and divided every few years, but it will take some digging, for the roots are substantial.

Comfrey

Symphytum officinale

Red flowers hang in pendant bunches from the axils of the upper leaves of this shade-tolerant lover of damp soils. Unless, that is, you find the white-flowered variety. Or the yellow/white-flowered one. Or the blue-flowered one, though that is a different species, *S. asperum* or rough comfrey, which used to be widely grown as a fodder crop for cattle. Its flowers are pink in bud, giving a two-tone effect like that of lungwort, though the plants are larger. Another close relative is the naturalized Russian comfrey, of which there are numerous garden varieties available, including compact versions and variegated ones such as goldsmith. Rough comfrey can take drier soils than the others, but all need room to spread. Their flowers are shown to excellent effect when grown on stream banks or pond edges, where the ground is banked so that a lower viewpoint is available. Flowering season is from May to July. Comfrey is also useful to the organic gardener, who can make a very good liquid feed from the leaves: allow them to rot down, compressed in a barrel for a few weeks, then draw off the resultant liquid and dilute it 1 part in 10 or 20 of water.

Height: 1m (3ft).

Habitat: Damp meadows, woodland, river banks and roadsides.

Garden care: Comfreys tolerate shade well but do not need it. What they do like is a damp soil and room to spread. Their large leaves can make a good contrast to ferns.

Propagation: Seed is available, as are plants, but the plants sold in most outlets are the varieties of Russian comfrey mentioned above. For the native plant, you need to go to more specialist nurseries. Plants older than two years can be dug up and divided in spring.

Cotton Grass *Eriophorum angustifolium*

This rhizomatous perennial is classed amongst the sedges, which lack the swollen joints of the true grasses and have a triangular cross-section to the stems. It forms sparse tufts of growth with stiffly erect stems and narrow, grooved leaves which are sharply pointed at the tips. The flower spikes are short-stalked, in groups of three to five. They tend to hang down slightly and are a brownish colour when in flower, the characteristic cottony bristles growing out after fertilization has occurred. Cotton grass flowers in April and May; the short tufts of cotton, which wave and shake in the breeze, follow from May and last well into the summer.

Height: Up to 50cm (20in).

Habitat: Bogs, pools and marshes, usually on acid or peaty soils. Enjoys full sun. Tolerant of neutral sub-soil or planting compost.

Garden care: Lift and divide every three years. Cut down dead stems as they appear, both for the sake of appearance and to prevent them from rotting in the water.

Propagation: Available from some nurseries and water garden centres. Divisions can be replanted when plants are cut back every three years. Seed heads can be potted in damp compost and sealed in a plastic bag until germination, when the bag can be removed and the plants grown on for planting out in the following spring.

Creeping Jenny *Lysimachia nummularia*

This highly adaptable plant could equally have been included in the chapter on rockery plants or the one on pond plants or the mixed border chapter. However, as it is usually found in damp places in the wild, here it is. One of our prettier natives, the straggling stems have opposite pairs of rounded, bright-green leaves and similar-sized, bright-yellow cup-shaped flowers from May well into July. The flowers grow on short stalks from the axils of the middle leaves, rather than towards the tips of the stems. If the conditions suit it – which most do – creeping Jenny can form a dense mat of foliage, spreading to about 60cm (24in) across. A golden-leafed variety, *L. n.* 'Aurea', is also widely available.

Height: About 5cm (2in).

Habitat: Grows naturally in damp meadows, wet woodland and ditches. Prefers semi-shade, but will tolerate full sun, in which case the leaves sometimes take on a reddish tinge. Can grow on the rockery, if the soil is fairly rich or plenty of organic matter is dug in before planting.

Garden care: Water in dry weather if placing in a rockery. Plants can be trimmed to size whenever it suits, and the trimmings used as cuttings if required. Dead-heading will extend the flowering season a little.

Propagation: Commonly available from garden centres and nurseries. Cuttings can be taken from non-flowering stems during the warmer months and rooted in pots of damp compost or even just a jar of water.

Figwort – Common

Scrophularia nodosa

The most common of three figworts native to Britain, the common figwort has rectangular stems with short-stalked leaves in opposite pairs and a very loose, very branched flower spike. The flowers are small and greenish brown with a red upper lip which stands out well against the sky or open water. It flowers from June to September and, although not spectacular, is remarked upon wherever it is seen in gardens. It looks very good in combination with the yellow flag (*Iris pseudacorus*) or yellow loosestrife (*Lysimachia vulgaris*), for example. One of the other native figworts is the water figwort (*S. auriculata*), of which there is a very attractive variegated form available from nurseries and the larger garden centres.

Height: Up to 1m (3ft).

Habitat: Wet woodlands, ditches and shaded stream banks.

Garden care: Dead-heading would be somewhat impractical with this one, but the flowering season lasts quite well anyway. A herbaceous perennial, it can be cut down to the base in late autumn.

Propagation: Plants and seed are available from specialist nurseries. Existing plants can be lifted and divided every three years or so, in spring or autumn.

Fleabane – Common

Pulicaria dysenterica

The branching, pale-green stems of this perennial bear wrinkled, downy oblong-to-lanceolate leaves of the same colour, the bases of which clasp the stems slightly. The tips of the stems carry bright-yellow, daisy-like flowers with large centres and short ray-florets from July into September. A very bright, decorative plant, contrasting well with darker specimens, like the water mint (*Mentha aquatica*) or some of the rushes. Its name comes from the Middle Ages and before, when it was burned to drive fleas away from houses, though the effectiveness of this is not clear and it certainly attracts its share and more of insects when in flower.

Height: Up to about 60cm (24in).

Habitat: Wet woodland, ditch banks and marshes. Grows in light or heavy soils, in sun or shade.

Garden care: Dead-heading will extend the flowering season. The plant can be cut down to near the base at the end of autumn.

Propagation: Available from specialist nurseries. Seed can be saved from existing plants in the garden and sown in pots in late summer, pressed into the surface of damp compost. Plants can be lifted and divided in spring or autumn.

Globe Flower   *Trollius europaeus*

The round, globular flowers of this tall perennial appear – and in a few cultivated varieties, open – between April and July at the tops of dark, slender stems. The flowers are usually golden yellow, though there are pale varieties as well as orange ones in cultivation, for this is a popular garden flower as well as a native plant. Often, they appear not to open at all, staying round and globular, but in varieties such as the one illustrated, the petals do lay back to reveal the upright spray of anthers. The lower leaves are stalked and palmate, while those above are unstalked, three-lobed and toothed around the margins, arranged around the upright, often dark-reddish stems.

Height: Up to 75cm (30in).

Habitat: Wet meadows, damp woods and stream-sides, mainly in the north and west of Britain. Thrives in sun or shade.

Garden care: Ensure when planting that the plant has a damp location and plenty of organic matter in the soil. Mulch in spring or autumn, water if there is any risk of the ground drying out in summer and cut back to ground level in autumn.

Propagation: Plants and seed are available from garden centres and nurseries. Existing plants can be lifted and divided every three years in spring or autumn.

Hemp Agrimony   *Eupatorium cannabinum*

Known as 'raspberries and cream' in Britain's West Country, this tall, reddish-stemmed perennial has downy leaves divided into three or five segments, each shaped like the head of a lance, with toothed margins. The stems are branched, with broad terminal clusters of tiny red, pink and white flowers from early July well into October. The leaves are a fairly dark green and are borne in opposite pairs on the stems. The plant extends the flowering season of the wetland garden beyond any of its compatriots, well into autumn. The double-flowered variety 'Flore Pleno' is available from some nurseries.

Height: Up to 1.2m (4ft), depending on where it is growing and with what.

Habitat: River banks, pond margins, wet woodland and ditches. Can tolerate sun or shade, dense or open planting.

Garden care: Mulch in spring with organic matter and cut flower heads back when they have finished. Stems can be cut back in early winter, when the plants have died back fully.

Propagation: Plants and seed are available from nurseries and some garden centres. Seed can be saved from existing plants and sown in pots of damp compost outside in autumn to germinate the following spring.

Lady's Smock
Cardamine pratensis

This pretty plant was once much more common than it is now. Also known as 'milkmaids' and 'cuckoo flower' in certain parts of England, it has pale-pink, four-petalled flowers, borne in a loose bunch at the top of the slender stem from April into June. The basal leaves are pinnate, or segmented, the segments small and rounded, in pairs, the tip leaflet larger, slightly toothed. The stem leaves are also pinnate, but the leaflets are narrow, almost linear, and the leaves do not have stalks. Lady's smock is a perennial plant, growing from a short rhizome.

Height: 20–40cm (8–16in).

Habitat: Damp meadows, wet woodland, stream-sides and shady lanes.

Garden care: Ensure that the roots do not dry out, cut back the stems in autumn, and lift and divide plants every three or four years in spring or autumn.

Propagation: Seed and plants are available from specialist nurseries. Seed can be saved from existing plants and sown in damp compost, the pots then sealed with cling film until germination has taken place. Plants can be divided every three or four years.

Loosestrife – Purple
Lythrum salicaria

This tall, majestic plant grows in wetlands throughout southern Britain, as far north as south-west Scotland. Charles Darwin discovered that there are, in fact, three forms, which are different in the length of their stamens and styles and do not interbreed, but they have never been given different specific names. The leaves of purple loosestrife are dark green and hairy, the lower ones borne in whorls of three, gradually giving way up the length of the sometimes-branched stem to alternate pairs of leaves and then to the flower spike. This may be well over 30cm (12in) long, made up of whorls of flowers, each up to 2.5cm (1in) across and a rich, reddish purple in colour, though there are violet, pink and white forms. The hairy stems of this rhizomatous perennial become woody with age and are definitely square in section. The flowering season is from July to September. Various garden cultivars are available, including ones with pale-pink and deep-red flowers.

Height: Commonly up to 1m (3ft), but can grow to as much as 2m (6ft), especially if shaded.

Habitat: Marshes, river and pond banks, ditches and wet meadows, though they can also flourish in drier conditions. A sunny position suits the plant best.

Garden care: Water in well when planting; remove flower spikes as they become spent, unless seed is required.

Propagation: Plants and seed are available from nurseries and some garden centres. Seed can be saved in autumn and sown fresh in pots or trays outdoors for planting out in the following spring. Plants can be lifted and divided every three years.

Loosestrife – Yellow *Lysimachia vulgaris*

In common with its close relatives, creeping Jenny (*L. nummularia*) and yellow pimpernel (*L. nemorum*), described elsewhere, yellow loosestrife is a very adaptable plant. It is an herbaceous perennial which grows upright from creeping horizontal basal stems that root at regular intervals along their length. The upright flowering stems are unbranched and have downy pointed leaves, about 6cm (2.5in) long near the base, getting smaller further up the stems. The cup-shaped, bright golden-yellow flowers are in loose panicles, at or near the tops of the stems. They are open through June and July. The plant will make a substantial tight stand in two or three years, bringing a splash of brightness to any border or bog garden. There is a very attractive variegated form also available from garden centres.

Height: Up to 1m (3ft), but usually around half that.

Habitat: In the wild, yellow loosestrife is found in wet woods, marshes, ditches and on river banks, but it will also grow well in drier places and can tolerate sun or shade, even growing and flowering well on a dry clay bank under trees.

Garden care: Water in well when planting and in really dry spells through the summer. Cut back flowering stems in autumn. Lift and divide every two or three years to keep the spreading habit in check.

Propagation: Commonly available in garden centres and nurseries, as plants or seeds. Seed should be sown in late spring or early summer in pots or trays outside, the young plants planted out in the following spring. Existing plants can be lifted and divided every two or three years.

Marigold – Marsh *Caltha palustris*

One of the earliest-flowering wetland plants, suitable for the bog garden or the shallow edges of the pond. It is commonly found in ditches, damp woods, marshes and stream-sides, where its large, golden-yellow flowers brighten a sunny or shady spot from early April until late May or June and can be persuaded to continue intermittently until August. They are borne on branching stems that rise above the large, heart-shaped leaves. Plants vary greatly in size, leaves ranging from 7.5–20cm (3–8in) across. Early leaves, before flowering, are always smaller than those during or after flowering. The flowers look like large buttercups and the leaves are finely toothed around the edges. There is a white-flowered form, *C. palustris* 'Alba', but this is less free-flowering than the original and a weaker plant. Also, a double form is available with the suffix 'Plena' or 'Flore Pleno' attached to its name.

Height: Up to 60cm (24in).

Habitat: Wet meadows, stream-sides and wet woodland. Ground must not dry out completely at any time of year, though the plant can tolerate full sun or partial shade.

Garden care: Best planted below the water line in the shallow part of a pond or in the bog garden. Dead-heading can extend the flowering season sporadically through the summer. Remove dead leaves through the summer and autumn before they rot.

Propagation: Seed or plants are available at garden centres and nurseries. Plants can be divided in summer, immediately after flowering.

Meadow Sweet   *Filipendula ulmaria*

You need to look closely at this substantial perennial to be able to tell which family it comes from, and then only when the flowers are fully open, for this sweet-smelling, foamy-headed plant is classified as a member of the rose family. The tall stems are dark reddish in colour and branched, the leaves dark green with greyish hairs underneath, divided into five to eleven segments, each roughly triangular and toothed at the margins. The tiny, five-petalled creamy flowers are carried in foamy heads towards the top of the plant from June to September, clumps of meadow sweet making a spectacular sight in damp meadows, ditches and stream-sides through the summer. There is a yellow-leaved variety available, *F. u.* 'Aurea'. Another, similar native species which grows on dry ground, often on limestone soils, is dropwort (*F. vulgaris*).

Height: Up to 2m (6ft) if drawn, but often around 1m (3ft).

Habitat: Damp meadows, stream-sides and open wet woodland. Thrives in sun or shade.

Garden care: Add organic matter to the soil when planting, mulch in spring, ensure the soil does not dry out in summer and cut down the stems in autumn.

Propagation: Plants are available from nurseries and garden centres. Existing plants in the garden can be lifted and divided in autumn or spring.

Mint – Water   *Mentha aquatica*

There are well over a dozen species growing in the wild in Britain that are classified as belonging to the mint family, including herbs such as marjoram (*Origanum vulgare*), basil (*Clinopodium vulgare*) and the thymes. Most of them, however, unlike water mint, like to grow in dry situations. This lightly hairy plant bears the characteristic smell of mint, especially when the short-stalked, oval leaves are rubbed between the fingers. It bears small, pink flowers in rounded terminal racemes from July into October.

Height: Up to 60cm (24in) if grown in shade or in close competition with other plants, but usually only about 20cm (8in).

Habitat: Stream banks, wet meadows, marshes and wet woodland. Will grow in sun or shade, in wet soil or actually in a few inches of water.

Garden care: Like many of the mints, this one needs to be restricted if it is not to spread widely, so is best grown in a container of some sort, or at least a confined space. Can be affected by rust disease. If this is seen, infected leaves should immediately be removed and destroyed.

Propagation: Plants available from garden centres and nurseries. Existing plants can be divided in spring or autumn.

Pimpernel – Bog

Anagalis tenella

Closely related to the scarlet pimpernel described in the rockery chapter, this creeping perennial has tiny pink flowers in abundance from May to August. These are funnel-shaped, with five petals and pale, almost-white, stamens. They are borne on 2.5cm (1in) stalks from the axils of the tiny, pale-green, smooth and shiny round leaves, which grow in opposite pairs from the straggling, pale stems. The plants sprawl among other plants over the surface of wet marshes or pond edges, forming tight mats which can become up to 12cm (5in) thick if other plants allow them to clamber up as well as across.

Height: Alone, up to 5cm (2in); with support, up to 12cm (5in).

Habitat: Boggy ground, wet marshes and pond edges, usually in sun.

Garden care: Trim to size if necessary in the growing season and cut back to the base of the stems in autumn.

Propagation: Plants are available from specialist nurseries. Cuttings can be taken in spring or summer and rooted in damp compost, or seed can be saved from plants in the garden and sown fresh in summer.

Ragged Robin

Lychnis flos-cuculi

Although its Latin name means 'cuckoo flower' and relates to the time of year when it starts to flower, this is not the plant commonly called the cuckoo flower, the unrelated lady's smock (*Cardamine pratensis*). The open pink flowers with their ragged-looking petals are borne in loose, branched bunches, mostly at the top of this red-stemmed perennial. The leaves are small, narrow and carried in opposite pairs, often tight to the branched stems and below the prominently displayed flowers. The flowers occur from May to August, though this can be extended another month by regular dead-heading. They are very attractive to bees and butterflies. There is also a white-flowered form available from some garden centres.

Height: Up to 60cm (24in).

Habitat: Marshes, damp meadows and wet woodland.

Garden care: Dead-head regularly to prolong the flowering period and cut down the old stems in autumn.

Propagation: Plants and seed are available from specialist nurseries. Seed can be saved from established plants and sown fresh in damp compost, outside. Plants should be lifted and divided every three years or so in spring or autumn, the divisions replanted and watered in well.

Rosebay Willowherb

Epilobium angustifolium

Named for its leaves, which are reminiscent of those of the willow trees, rosebay willowherb is one of several closely related species native to Britain. It has long terminal spikes of pink flowers, the four broad petals often divided from each other by the darker, purplish sepals, which are retained after the flower opens. The stamens are prominent and white, giving a hint of what is to come after the flower fades. The seed capsule and the seed bear long, downy hairs which give the plant an autumn appearance of having a thick, silvery coat of hair. Unlike the purple loosestrife (*Lythrum salicaria*), the willowherb stem is not branched and the long, narrow leaves, carried in a spiral arrangement up the stem, are smooth. Also known as fireweed and French willow, this is a very

adaptable plant and a quick colonizer, the wind carrying its seed into areas of felling in forests and into the rubble of destroyed buildings. Its close relative, the broad-leaved willowherb (*E. montanum*) is a common weed of gardens, having shorter, broader leaves and much less significant flowers. Great willowherb (*E. hirsutum*) is a sturdier-looking plant of similar height to rosebay willowherb, with larger but far fewer flowers distributed occasionally up the stem and in a loose group among the leaves at the top of the plant. Almost as common as rosebay willowherb and growing in similar situations, it is far less garden-worthy. There is a white-flowered variety of rosebay willowherb which is very attractive.

Height: Up to 1.5m (5ft).

Habitat: Clearings, footpaths, road sides, waste ground and river and lake banks.

Garden care: Dead-head thoroughly through the flowering season, which lasts from June to September, and cut down the stems to ground level in autumn. Lift and divide the plants every three years or so, digging in plenty of organic matter when replanting to encourage flowering.

Propagation: Seed and plants are available from specialist nurseries. Seed can be saved and sown in pots or trays in late summer to be planted out the following spring. Plants can be lifted and the rhizomatous stock divided every three or four years.

Soft Rush

Juncus effusus

One of the most common of nearly thirty species of rush that grow wild in Britain, the soft rush – like the vast majority of rushes – grows in wet places such as bogs and pond edges. There are two groups of rushes, which differ in where on the stem the flower cluster is held: the soft rush belongs to the group whose flowers are found part-way down the stem, rather than clustered at the top. It has a loose panicle, about 2.5cm (1in) across and yellowish green. Flowering is from early June to September. The pith-filled stems are the same dark green as the hollow, tubular leaves. It forms dense evergreen clumps, up to 30cm (12in) across, providing good colour contrast to paler-leaved or bright-flowered plants. There is a form of this plant whose stems spiral loosely known as the corkscrew rush, with the suffix 'Spiralis' on the name. This looks very effective against a pale background, especially when planted close to the corkscrew hazel (*Corylus avellana* 'Spiralis'), another rare form of a native plant recently popular in garden centres.

Height: Usually 30-60cm (12–24in)

Habitat: Damp grassland, bogs and wet woodland. Can grow in sun or shade. A tough plant which will squeeze out competing plants from its space.

Garden care: Lift and divide clumps every two or three years. Pull out dead stems to keep the plant looking its best. Remove flower spikes when over to prevent seed setting, unless it is required for propagation.

Propagation: Plants sometimes found in garden centres and nurseries. Existing plants can be lifted and divided every two or three years; or seed can be saved and sown in pots outside in wet compost, sealed in a plastic bag until germination has taken place.

Spearwort – Lesser *Ranunculus flammula*

The two native spearworts are very similar, except for their sizes. Both have long, slender leaves, pointed at both ends. Both have buttercup-like flowers from April to June. The greater spearwort (*R. lingua*) will grow in open water, while the lesser tends to be more of a marshland plant. The main difference, though, is in size. The lesser spearwort has flowers 2.5cm (1in) across and grows up to 60cm (24in) tall, whereas the greater is around twice as big. Both are very attractive plants, both to us and to hoverflies and other insects.

Height: Up to 60cm (24in).

Habitat: Marshes, fens and ditches, often in full sun. Can tolerate close planting.

Garden care: Like most of the buttercup family, the spearworts have poisonous sap, so wearing gloves is advisable when handling them. Dead-heading will extend the flowering season. The plants can be cut down at the end of the growing season.

Propagation: Plants are available from nurseries and water garden centres, though the greater spearwort is more commonly available. Existing plants can be lifted and divided in spring, or seed can be saved and sown in pots of damp compost in summer. This is best done when the seed is as fresh as possible.

Wood Small-reed *Calamagrostis epigeios*

This tough perennial grows from long rhizomes. The dark, greyish-green leaves are long, stiff and rough. They roll up almost in the manner of a rush in dry conditions, but flatten out again when the plant is watered. The flower panicle is large and dense, even when in flower during June, July and August. Also called bush grass, this darkly handsome plant grows naturally at the edges of woods, in ditches and scrubland and on wet ground, often in the shade. It forms large clumps if allowed to, but is well worth using in a cultivated setting as a background to brighter subjects, as well as in its own right.

Height: Usually 1m (3ft), but can achieve twice that.

Habitat: Wet ground, often in shade, though it can tolerate a sunny site.

Garden care: Lift and divide every two years to keep clumps to a useful size as well as making more plants, if required.

Propagation: Seed is available from specialist nurseries or can be saved from existing plants and sown in damp compost sealed in a plastic bag until germination.

Woundwort – Marsh   *Stachys palustris*

There are three species of woundwort in Britain, the other one that is commonly found being hedge woundwort (*S. sylvatica*). This has a longer, more slender and more sparse flower spike, usually of a rich, deep red, though there is a pink variety available. Also related are the grey, woolly, pink-flowered lamb's ears (*S. lantana*) and the native herb betony (*S. officinalis*). Marsh woundwort is a tall, slender plant which looks very like a large mint, with slender, lance-shaped leaves carried in pairs on very short stalks from the square main stem. The pink mint-like flowers, 1.5cm (0.5in) long, are carried in a dense spike at the top of the plant from mid June into September.

Height: 60–100cm (2–3ft).

Habitat: Wet meadows, marshes and river banks.

Garden care: An organic feed in spring will encourage the plant to do well in summer, as well as lightening the soil, which it will welcome. Flower spikes can be cut back when they have finished to encourage more flowering and the whole plant cut down to the base later in autumn.

Propagation: Plants and seed are available from nurseries and some water garden centres. Clumps can be lifted and divided in spring every three years or so.

MARSH AND BOG PLANTS

	HEIGHT	FLOWERING SEASON	FLOWER COLOUR
Avens – Water	1m (3ft)	May–June	Orange
Bedstraw – Marsh	60cm (24in)	June–Sept	White
Bird's-foot Trefoil – Greater	75cm (30in)	June–Aug	Yellow
Bog Asphodel	30cm (12in)	July–Aug	Yellow
Butterbur	1m (3ft)	March–May	Pink
Comfrey	1m (3ft)	May–Aug	Red/white
Cotton Grass	50cm (20cm)	April–May	Brown
Creeping Jenny	5cm (2in)	May–July	Yellow
Figwort – Common	1m (3ft)	June–Sept	Red
Fleabane – Common	60cm (24in)	July–Sept	Yellow
Globe Flower	75cm (30in)	April–July	Yellow
Hemp Agrimony	1.2m (4ft)	July–Oct	White/pink
Lady's Smock	40cm (16in)	April–June	Pink
Loosestrife – Purple	2m (6ft)	July–Sept	Purple
Loosestrife – Yellow	1m (3ft)	June–July	Yellow
Marigold – Marsh	60cm (24in)	April–Aug	Yellow
Meadow Sweet	2m (6ft)	June–Sept	White
Mint – Water	60cm (24in)	July–Oct	Mauve
Pimpernel – Bog	12cm (5in)	May–Aug	Pink
Ragged Robin	60cm (24in)	May–Aug	Pink
Rosebay Willowherb	1.2m (4ft)	July–Sept	Pink
Soft Rush	60cm (24in)	June–Sept	Yellow/green
Spearwort – Lesser	60cm (24in)	April–June	Yellow
Wood Small-reed	1m (3ft)	June–Aug	Cream
Woundwort – Marsh	1m (3ft)	June–Sept	Pink

Chapter Five

❖

Pond Plants

POND PLANTS

A<small>NY GARDEN</small> is so much poorer without water that some form of pond or water feature is almost essential. Its calming influence is renowned: the sound of running water, be it a stream or a simple bubble fountain, is so relaxing. A pond can be anything from a small pebble bowl or millstone with a pump and a little fountain to a large pond with fish and plants creating its own little habitat. Few of us are fortunate enough to have a stream at the bottom of the garden or to

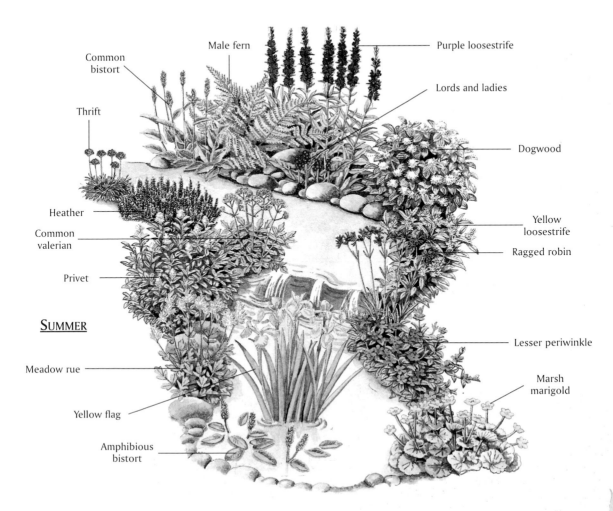

Common bistort

Male fern

Purple loosestrife

Lords and ladies

Thrift

Dogwood

Heather

Yellow loosestrife

Common valerian

Ragged robin

Privet

SUMMER

Lesser periwinkle

Meadow rue

Marsh marigold

Yellow flag

Amphibious bistort

live next to the village pond, so any water feature in our gardens will have to be artificial. There are many ways of creating a water garden: it may be formal or natural, raised or sunken, with or without fish or frogs or other wildlife. The one thing that is essential is some form of sealed container. Any container, large or small, rigid or flexible, can be adapted to make a water feature. Some plants can be kept quite happily in a half-barrel with a pump to move the water around so that it does not stagnate. Others need a large area to spread into in order to give of their best.

All ponds need either a pump or some oxygenating plants – preferably both. But such plants are not restricted to Canadian pondweed and its relatives, which quickly become a nuisance by growing far too prolifically. There are also native plants such as the water violet (*Hottonia palustris*) and spiked water milfoil

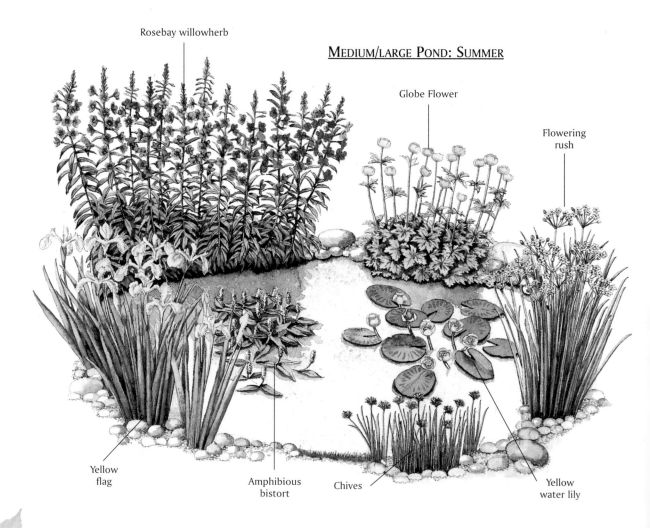

Rosebay willowherb

MEDIUM/LARGE POND: SUMMER

Globe Flower

Flowering rush

Yellow flag

Amphibious bistort

Chives

Yellow water lily

(*Myriophyllum spicatum*), which are much less vigorous and just as effective, though they are not quite so easy to come by. There are floating plants such as the water soldier (*Stratiotes aloides*) and frogbit (*Hydrocharis morsus-ranae*), or shallow-water plants like the fringed water lily (*Nymphoides peltata*), water forget-me-not (*Myosotis scorpioides*) and water speedwell (*Veronica anagallis-aquatica*) and several others. Then there are deep-water plants such as the water lilies. Or, for a little bubble fountain, you can use plants that simply like a damp atmosphere, such as ferns and hostas (for a strictly native garden hostas can be replaced with cuckoo pint (*Arum maculatum*) or comfrey (*Symphytum officinale*). All have their own place in the pond and there are few plants out there which could be said to be not worth having, given that your pond is suitable for them. It is simply a matter of scale and aesthetics to choose plants that will suit the size and style of pond you wish to create. Then it is down to the hard work of digging or building, lining it, filling it, arranging the pump and probably a filter of some kind, letting it settle and introducing the plants you have selected. Once they have established themselves, then wildlife will move in of its own accord and you may find frogs, toads and damsel flies populating your garden. Birds may drink from the feature or bathe in it, and night animals such as hedgehogs and foxes may do the same. There is nothing like good, clean water in the garden to bring out the best in it.

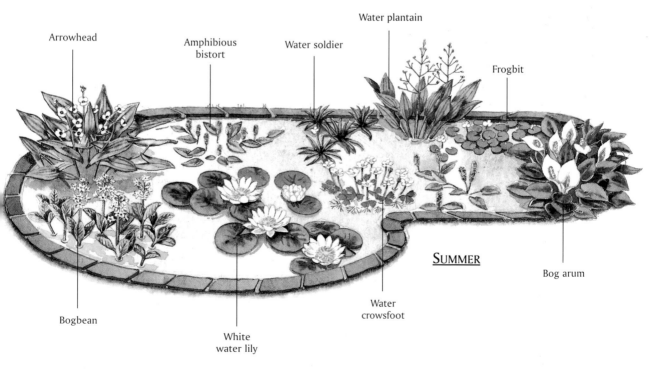

Water plantain

Arrowhead

Amphibious bistort

Water soldier

Frogbit

SUMMER

Bog arum

Bogbean

Water crowsfoot

White water lily

Amphibious Bistort

Polygonum amphibium

This plant takes two forms, depending upon whether it is growing on land or in the water. In the water, where it is usually seen, it is a hairless plant with long, twining stems. On land, however, it has shorter stems and smaller, hairy leaves. The leaves of the aquatic form are up to 20cm (8in) long, slender and oval in shape, mid-green in colour on 4cm (1.5in) stalks. The flowers, which occur from June to September, are tiny and pink, carried in tight spikes up to 10cm (4in) long, held upright above the water surface.

Height: 10cm (4in) in flower. Spread: indefinite, rooting at the leaf nodes if they touch the bottom, in the shallows.

Habitat: Usually fairly shallow water up to 45cm (18in) deep, in ponds, ditches and lakes.

Garden care: Cut back when it gets too large and when the leaves begin to yellow. A plant for the larger pond, where it will have room to spread. Cannot really give of its best in a small space.

Propagation: Available from nurseries and water garden centres. Divide plants in spring.

Arrowhead

Sagittaria sagittifolia

Named for the shape of its upright, long-stalked leaves, this is a close relative of the water plantain (*Alisma plantago-aquatica*). The first leaves to appear in spring from this sturdy perennial are grass-like, up to 1m (3ft) long and floating in the water. Then come the upright, triangular stems, each with its arrowhead leaf up to 30cm (12in) long. Lastly come the branching flower stems, up to 30cm (12in) above the surface of the water, with three-petalled white male flowers with black centres being carried above the spherical black buttons of the female flowers on the stems. These are carried from mid June well into August.

Height: Up to 1m (3ft) above the water surface.

Habitat: Ponds, canals and slow-flowing rivers in water up to 60cm (24in) deep. Flowers better in water 15cm (6in) deep or less. Requires full sun.

Garden care: Cut away leaves as they die back through the season. Cut down flowering stem when it has finished. If done quickly this will encourage further flowering later in the season. Cut back leaves to the base after they have died back in early winter.

Propagation: Plants are available from nurseries and garden centres. Existing plants can be divided in spring or summer or new plantlets can be broken off in spring.

Arum – Bog
Calla palustris

This plant grows wild in a few lowland areas of Britain. It looks very much like a broader, shorter version of lords and ladies, or cuckoo pint (*Arum maculatum*), which is a widespread woodland plant. Its leaves are broad and rounded, the veins sweeping around towards their sharply pointed tips. The white spathe is shaped very much like the leaves and is quite open, backing rather than surrounding the thick flower stalk. The plant flowers through the summer from May to August, the flowers finally being replaced in autumn by the spikes of bright-red berries. The leaves can be evergreen in mild winters, but a prolonged cold snap will make them die back, only to regrow in the spring before the flowers open.

Height: Up to 30cm (12in). Similar spread, effected by rhizome growth.

Habitat: Pools, river shallows and boggy ground, either on peat bogs or in wet woodland. Can tolerate sun or shade, acid or neutral soil, but prefers shallow water.

Garden care: Keep away from children as the plant, including the very pretty berries, is poisonous. Cut away dead leaves in winter before they rot. Trim to size if necessary in spring.

Propagation: Plants available from nurseries and garden centres. Sections of rhizome can be cut away in spring and potted in wet compost to develop a good root system. The berries can be picked and sown in compost to germinate over winter, putting up new plants by late spring.

Bladderwort
Utricularia vulgaris

One of our native carnivorous plants, this is probably the least obvious of them. With finely divided leaves spreading through the water it has no roots, so floats at or near the surface. The leaves carry small bladders with hairy edges which trap and digest insects to help nourish the plant. The branching stems can be up to 1m (3ft) long, but are usually about half to a third of that. Reddish flower stems begin to rise vertically out of the water in June, each carrying several bright-yellow flowers from then into August. The plant is deciduous, dying back in winter and, like frogbit (*Hydrocharis morsus-ranae*), small buds fall to the bottom to overwinter, germinating into new plants in spring.

Height: Flower stems up to 30cm (12in) above the surface. Spread up to 1m (3ft).

Habitat: Ponds and lakes, in sun or shade, in water 15–100cm (6–36in) deep.

Garden care: None needed once established, except for perhaps cutting off the flower stems when they have finished.

Propagation: Plants are available from nurseries and some water garden centres. Cuttings can be taken in spring or summer.

Bogbean

Menyanthes trifoliata

Although for most of the year the plant is recognizable only by the trifoliate leaves growing out from its thick, creeping stem, in May and June it decorates itself with leafless stems bearing spikes of numerous pink or white flowers, opening from rosy red buds. The five petals of these are fringed very prettily at the edges and surround violet anthers. Although the display does not last that long relative to some other plants, it is well worth growing the plant for that alone – in the same way as many people grow magnolias just for the two or three weeks of the year when they flower – even without the attractive leaves. The leaves are borne on stalks up to 12cm (5in) long and each is divided into three very definite smooth, oval leaflets. The creeping main stem can become quite long, spreading as far as you will allow it.

Height: Up to 30cm (12in). Spread: indefinite.

Habitat: Ponds and the wettest parts of marshes.

Garden care: The leaves are deciduous, so will need to be removed once they die back in autumn. The plant can be cut back to size at this time or in the spring. These cuttings can be used, if taken while the plant is still growing, to make further plants by potting up in wet compost. If growing in a marshy area rather than a pond, watch for slug and snail damage and take the usual preventative measures. Rarely, the plant may be affected by powdery mildew. If this is seen, affected tissue must be removed and destroyed immediately.

Propagation: Plants are available from nurseries and good garden centres, especially places specializing in water gardening. Cuttings can be taken in the warmer months, as described above.

Bur-reed – Branched

Sparganium erectum

Sword-shaped leaves up to 1.5cm (0.5in) wide rise from the thick rhizomes of this sturdy perennial. Robust stems grow between them, topped in summer by stiff, branching panicles of spherical balls of yellow-green flowers from June to August, followed by tightly packed bunches of tiny brown nutlets where the female flower heads – the lower ones in the panicle – were. This is not a showy plant, but sufficiently different to be interesting in the garden when planted in association with reedmace (*Typha* sp.) or yellow flag (*Iris pseudacorus*).

Height: Up to 1.2m (4ft).

Habitat: Shallow water at the edges of ponds, streams or lakes; also in wet marshland.

Garden care: Can be susceptible to iris leaf spot, a fungal disease which is best dealt with by removing and destroying affected leaves as soon as it is noticed. Otherwise a very hardy plant, needing little care beyond making sure that it is placed in a suitable position in sun or semi-shade.

Propagation: Plants are available from some nurseries and water garden centres. Existing plants can be lifted and divided in spring or summer. Seed can be saved and sown in pots of wet compost in late summer.

Forget-me-not – Water

Myosotis scorpioides

With its stem growing along the ground, sending out runners and rooting itself as it goes, this pretty little plant decorates the shady shallows of ponds, lakes, streams and rivers throughout the British Isles with its brilliant blue flowers from May right through into September. Although it roots from the stem as it runs, it never becomes a large plant or a nuisance, for if it reaches places where it is not required, it is a simple task to pull it up and cut it back. With larger, brighter flowers than the other nine species of forget-me-not growing in Britain, it is well worth including in any water garden feature.

Height: About 15cm (6in).

Habitat: Shallow water, up to 15cm (6in), usually in shade.

Garden care: This little perennial is surprisingly tough, but can occasionally fall victim to botrytis, or grey mould disease. If this happens, remove all affected tissue as soon as possible and burn or discard it. Dead-heading will encourage a further flush of flowers.

Propagation: Plants are available from nurseries and garden centres. In the garden, clumps can be divided in spring or seed can be saved and sown in damp compost in summer.

Fringed Water Lily   *Nymphoides peltata*

Related to the bogbean (*Menyanthes trifoliata*) rather than the water lilies, this floating plant looks like a miniature water lily until you look closely. Then you find that it does not rise from the bottom of the pond but instead has trailing stems at or near the surface, which root from the leaf axils. The leaves are rounded with the indented base of the water lily, but only 4cm (1.5in) across, light green on the upper surface, reddish beneath. The bright-yellow flowers rise up on stalks 5cm (2in) above the water surface, the five petals opening to about 5cm (2in) across through June, July and August.

Height: 5cm (2in). Spread: 60cm (24in).

Habitat: Still water up to 45cm (18in) deep in sun or shade.

Garden care: Can be affected by leaf spot, as can water lilies. Remove affected leaves immediately and discard. Trim stems back to size if necessary, though it never gets to be a very large plant.

Propagation: Plants are available from nurseries and garden centres. Existing plants can be propagated by division in spring.

Frogbit
Hydrocharis morsus-ranae

Looking at first glance like a tiny water lily, the leaves of this plant are just 4cm (1.5in) across, on stems only about twice as long as the leaves themselves. These grow from a central bud, along with pale, trailing roots. The whole plant floats free in the water and is never more than 12cm (5in) across. Very rarely, it will flower, male and female flowers being on separate plants, with three white petals and a yellow centre. The flower is a little over 2.5cm (1in) across and held up 2.5cm (1in) or so above the surface. The flowering season is from June into August. In winter, the leaves are lost and the remaining bud sinks to survive the cold weather in the mud at the bottom, along with other buds produced vegetatively from the roots. In spring, these grow leaves and roots and rise to the surface again.

Height: About 6cm (2.5in), all of which is at or below the water surface.

Habitat: Sheltered standing water.

Garden care: Allow this pretty little plant to float free on shallow water and it will help to provide shade for fish, but watch for snail damage.

Propagation: Plants are available from some nurseries and water garden centres, though not reliably. As flowering is not common, reproduction is usually by vegetative budding from the roots in autumn.

Needle Spike Rush
Eleocharis acicularis

Sold in garden centres and nurseries as hair grass, this is a totally different plant from that delicate and pretty meadow plant. Tufts of fine, light-green leaves, rolled like the other spike rushes, grow to about 30cm (12in) long from roots in the bottom of ponds up to 60cm (24in) deep. An evergreen plant, it produces oxygen from the leaves – as do all plants – which helps to keep the water fresh: it is sold for this purpose as an alternative to the ubiquitous Canadian pondweed. It is much prettier and less of a nuisance in the pond, though somewhat less effective on its own.

Height: 30cm (12in).

Habitat: Ponds and lake shallows.

Garden care: Little care is needed, beyond splitting the clumps every three years or so, before they break their planting baskets. Set the plants at a maximum depth of 60cm (24in), though it looks very good growing from a depth of about 20cm (8in), where it is deep enough to survive the winter freeze, yet shallow enough for the blades to lean and drift in the water.

Propagation: Plants available from garden centres and nurseries. Can be lifted and divided every three years.

Pond Sedge – Greater *Carex riparia*

This robust tufted perennial with long, creeping rhizomes is a plant for the larger pond, unless the gardener has the time and inclination to lift it every couple of years and chop it back to size. However, it is a handsome plant with stiff, upright, bluish-green leaves which grow anywhere up to 1.5m (5ft) high. The flowering spikes can cover anything up to a third of the length of the stem. There are three to six closely packed male spikes near the top of the stem and about the same number of thicker, dark-green female spikes arranged down the stem. The upper one of these is stalkless and upright, while the lower ones have short stalks and droop away from the main stem. The flowers are displayed through May and June, fruiting following on until September. In common with many of the sedges that grow in water, the greater pond sedge dies back in winter.

Height: Up to 1.5m (5ft).

Habitat: Ponds and lakesides, streams and woodland marshes.

Garden care: Plant between 10–30cm (4–12in) deep, near the edge of the pond. Lift and divide every two years to keep the plant down to size. Cut back dead stems in winter before they rot.

Propagation: Plants are available from some nurseries. Divisions can be replanted in pond compost in baskets lined with hessian when the plant is cut back to size every couple of years. Pond compost is made up of mainly clay, with very little nutrient value in order to maintain the freshness of the pond and not encourage algal growth.

Reedmace – Common *Typha latifolia*

Found in streams and at lakesides, this plant is often wrongly called the bulrush. In suitable circumstances it can reach 3m (9ft) high, but is more usually 1–2m (3–6ft) high. It forms a dense cluster of large, grass-like foliage, from the base of which rise flowering stems with the typical rich-brown cylindrical spikes of tiny flowers. The female flowers are towards the base of the cigar-shaped inflorescence, which can be up to 30cm (12in) long. A smaller variant of this species, dwarf reedmace (*T. l.* 'Minima'), is sold in garden centres and nurseries for garden use. Similar to its larger relative in every other way, it reaches just 1.2m (4ft) tall, so is excellent for the smaller pond.

Height: Up to 3m (9ft) but more usually 1–2m (3–6ft).

Habitat: Streams and lakesides on light soil, in water up to 1.2m (4ft) deep.

Garden care: A plant for the larger pond, it will need dividing every two or three years to keep it in check, but nevertheless reedmace is a bold, stylish plant in the right situation. Likes a light, sandy growing medium. Best kept in a pond basket lined with hessian.

Propagation: Plants can be bought from nurseries or garden centres. From then on, propagate by division.

Reed Sweet-grass   *Glyceria maxima*

This rhizomatous perennial is often seen growing in large stands on the rich mud of stream and lake sides, often in deeper water than other species. It grows 1–2.1m (3–7ft) tall, the long, broad leaves strongly keeled along the underside of the mid-rib. The flower panicle can be up to 45cm (18in) long and has many erect, spreading branches. It is pale whitish-green at first, ageing to purple through a pink stage so that the three colours intermix in a stand of plants in a very pretty manner. The flowering period is from June into August. It is a plant for the larger pond and, even there, will need cutting back every couple of years to keep it in check or it will spread extensively.

Height: Up to 2.1m (7ft).

Habitat: Stream and lake margins, growing out into the water. Likes a sunny situation but is tolerant of most soils.

Garden care: A soil deep enough to take a substantial root system is needed, as this is a tall plant and therefore needs to anchor itself well. Cut back clumps to a manageable size every two or three years.

Propagation: Divisions can be replanted when cutting back or seed can be saved and sown in wet compost in late summer. Plants are sometimes available from specialist nurseries.

Rush – Flowering   *Butomus umbellatus*

One of our most attractive rushes, with tall, dark-green, narrow leaves and 10cm (4in) heads of pink flowers like a very loose allium head throughout the summer. This is an excellent plant for the garden pond as, like many of the rushes, it forms a tight clump, rather than spreading as many of the reeds are inclined to do. In fact, this decorative perennial is more closely related to the lilies and orchids than to other rushes. The family also contains the arums, reedmace and, believe it or not, common duckweed.

Height: Up to 1m (3ft).

Habitat: Ditches and pond margins. Shallow, slow-flowing or still water.

Garden care: Plant in shallow water up to 20cm (8in) deep, in a clay-type compost suitable for aquatic use. Remove faded flower heads through the summer, and cut off dead leaves in winter when they begin to droop. Very few disease problems will be encountered, but if signs of rust are seen remove affected leaves down to the base as soon as it is noticed.

Propagation: Plants are available from a wide range of aquatic and wildflower nurseries and some of the larger garden centres. Lift and divide plants in late summer, after flowering has finished. These plants are rhizomatous, like the border irises.

RUSHES

Common Spike-rush

Eleocharis palustris

Like the other rushes, this evergreen perennial is a clump-former, with leaves that are rolled into a tubular form up to 60cm (24in) long and stiffly upright. It spreads by means of long, creeping rhizomes. The cylindrical spikelets of flowers form brown heads at the tips of the stems, decorated with many yellow anthers from May to July. The common spike-rush grows in marshes, ditches and pond margins. It is one of several spike-rushes found growing wild in Britain, but is the most decorative.

Bog Rush

Schoenus nigricans

Similar in overall appearance to the common spike-rush, the bog rush grows in dense tufts. The thin, stiff stems actually bear very small, bristle-shaped leaf blades, giving away the bog rush's relationship to the sedges rather than the true rushes. The flower head is carried at the tip of the stem and is narrow, spindle-shaped and rust-coloured, bearing slightly less prominent whitish anthers in May and June. It is a plant of marshes and pond edges.

Compact Rush

Juncus conglomeratus

Also known as the conglomerate rush, this densely tufted perennial has finely striated stems, quite rough and matt green in colour with a continuous spongy pith in the centre, similar in many ways to the soft rush (*J. effusus*) mentioned elsewhere. Like the spike rush, the compact rush carries its inflorescence part-way down the stem, but in this case it is tight, rounded and dark brown, again flowering from May to July and naturally living in bogs, and also wet woodland and damp pasture.

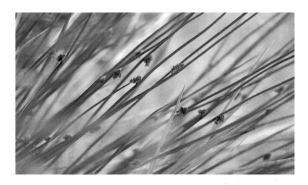

Thread Rush

Juncus filiformis

As the name suggests, the thread rush has very fine stems, growing up to 45cm (18in) long from creeping rhizomes. The brown flowers are surrounded by a whitish perianth, giving the loose inflorescence a pale, whitish overall appearance. The flower head appears about halfway down the stem in July and August. The thread rush is one of our less common rushes. It grows well in damp, poor soil, often on stony lake shores.

97

Spearwort – Greater _Ranunculus lingua_

Very similar from a distance to the lesser spearwort
(_R. flammula_) described in the chapter on wetland plants, the
greater spearwort is larger and more often found in standing
water, near the banks of ponds and streams. Like its cousin,
it has lanceolate, pale-green leaves held close to the stems
and bears bright-yellow buttercup-like flowers at the tops of
the stems throughout the summer. These are up to 5cm (2in)
across. This is a very showy plant when placed in front of
something more subtly coloured, such as reedmaces.

Height: Up to 1.2m (4ft).

Habitat: Shallow water.

Garden care: Buttercups are among the most resilient of our
native plants. Placed in a suitable situation, little should be able
to go wrong with them. Dead-head as the flowers finish to
encourage production of more later and cut back hard at the end
of the growing season, remembering to wear gloves as a
precaution because they have poisonous sap.

Propagation: Plants are available from nurseries and garden
centres. Seed can be saved from existing plants and sown fresh
on damp compost outside in late summer. Plants can be divided
in spring or autumn, every three years.

Speedwell – Water

Veronica anagallis-aquatica

One of eighteen species of speedwell native to Britain. Unlike
most, but in common with marsh speedwell (_V. scutellata_), it
has long, narrow, lanceolate leaves. The flower spikes grow
up from the axils of the topmost pair of leaves. In the case of
marsh speedwell, only one spike grows up from each stem,
the flowers a pinkish colour. In water speedwell, however,
two flower spikes are formed from each stem and the
flowers are of the more typical blue, appearing from May
through to October. Each flower is little more than the size
of a forget-me-not flower, the spike being around 7.5cm (3in)
long. Also closely related and available from water garden
outlets is brooklime (_V. beccabunga_), which has dark-blue,
white-centred flowers in short spikes above shiny-green,
oblong leaves.

Height: Up to about 15cm (6in) above the water surface when
in flower.

Habitat: Shallow parts of ponds and streams.

Garden care: In common with several of its relatives, this is a
semi-evergreen plant, dying back only in particularly harsh
weather. Dead-heading will encourage bushiness and more
flower spikes later in the season.

Propagation: Plants are available from nurseries and water
garden centres. The wetland speedwells can be propagated from
seed, summer cuttings or by division.

Starwort
Callitriche palustris

This extremely variable little plant has been called the chameleon of the water plants. It will grow in up to 60cm (24in) of water or on the pond margin, where it can form a mound of mossy foliage up to 15cm (6in) high. Beneath the surface, the stems are long and slender, with narrow leaves paired at the joints, from where fine floating roots also develop. Above the surface the stems shorten and the leaves widen into an almost circular shape, forming little rosettes. The flowers are tiny, greenish-white stars, appearing from May to September on the sections above the water surface.

Height: Below the surface, up to 60cm (24in); on the pond edge, 15cm (6in). Spreads to 45cm (18in).

Habitat: Still or flowing water, growing from the pond or stream bottom or on the edge of the water.

Garden care: Clip surface growth back in autumn to a few centimetres under the water: otherwise the frost will do the same and make a sloppy mess in the process. Trim to size when necessary.

Propagation: Available from specialist nurseries and water garden centres. Plants in the garden can be lifted and divided every two or three years or pieces about 7.5cm (3in) long, with some water roots on, can be cut off and potted up in wet compost to make new plants.

Water Cress
Nasturtium officinale

This hairless perennial is the spicy, dark-leaved plant of the salad bowl. If it is seen growing wild it should be washed thoroughly in clean water before being eaten, in case of water-born parasites, which it tends to harbour. It bears small white flowers in a flattened cluster from early June through to September above leaves which are divided pinnately, i.e. into definite segments, each with its own central rib coming off the main rib of the leaf, in the same way as the leaves of roses are divided. The clusters of flowers are about 4cm (1.5in) across, standing out brightly in a shady spot in the shallows of a pond. A related species, winter cress (*N. microphyllum*), is also cultivated and crossed with water cress to produce a late-harvesting variety for salads. Both produce long, thin seed pods similar to those of their relatives, the wallflowers.

Height: 60cm (24in).

Habitat: Shallow ponds and streams, also marshy areas, especially on chalk or limestone.

Garden care: Not suited to acidic or peaty areas, but will thrive in sun or shade. Sunny spots produce better leaves for the table, but in shade the flowers give a useful bright spot. Dead-heading, if the plant is placed where it can be reached, will prolong flowering.

Propagation: Plants are available from a few nurseries. Commercially, the plant is propagated by cuttings in summer, but once you have the plant, you can harvest and sow the seed. Naturally, the plant spreads by creeping rhizomes.

Water Crowfoot   *Ranunculus aquatilis*

One of several very similar species native to Britain, including the river water crowfoot (*R. fluitans*), this ferny-leaved perennial covers itself with white buttercup flowers from late April well into June. Closely related to the buttercups, the most important difference between those and the water crowfoots is that the latter are not poisonous: indeed, they are palatable and nutritious. The plants grow mostly submerged, usually in the shallower parts of ponds and lakes. The leaves are finely divided and can be up to 1m (3ft) long, making the plant quite substantial. In late spring floating leaves develop, along with flowering stems whose buds open into yellow-centred white flowers about 2cm (0.75in) across. Definitely a plant for the larger pond, it is still well worth the space it takes up in early summer.

Height: Grows in water to about 60cm (24in) deep. Spread: up to 1.2m (4ft).

Habitat: Still water, in sun or shade. Will grow in moving water, but will not flower.

Garden care: Cut back to required size when it gets too large. Dead-head when flowering is finished.

Propagation: Plants are available from some specialist nurseries. Seed can be saved from existing plants and sown in damp compost, covered so that it will not dry out. Clumps can be lifted and divided every two or three years.

Water Lily – White *Nymphaea alba*

This lovely flower is often grown in garden ponds, but has only two cultivated varieties other than the natural one – a pink-flowered one and a small-flowered one. The other water lilies grown in our gardens are generally of foreign origin, often oriental. The many petals of the white water lily open to a cup shape during the day, revealing the rich-yellow boss of stamens at their centre until evening, when the flower closes and can sink below the water surface to re-emerge the following morning. Both flowers and round leaves float on the surface of still or slow-flowing water up to 3m (9ft) deep, the stalks growing up from large rhizomatous basal stems in the mud of the bottom. The scented flowers can be 20cm (8in) across and are displayed from May to August. The large leaves are deeply cut at the base, to where the stem joins. They are almost circular, reddish on the underside with a green upper surface and a leathery texture. They dot the surface of the pond through most of the spring, summer and autumn, dying back in winter.

Height: Can grow in a water depth of up to 3m (9ft), the floating flowers being up to 10cm (4in) high.

Habitat: Ponds, lakes and slow-moving streams or rivers.

Garden care: Plant in a basket to restrict growth. Lift and trim to size every couple of years. Trimmings can be used as cuttings to start new plants. Can be attacked by a fungal disease called brown spot, which causes dark blotches on the leaves. Infected leaves should be cut away from the base immediately and burned. As a preventative measure old, yellowing leaves should be removed promptly and the water kept fresh and healthy. Water lily beetle can occasionally attack plants, leaving patches or wriggling trails of holes in the leaves. Adult beetles can also attack the flowers. The beetles hibernate over winter in poolside vegetation, so cutting this back in late autumn will help, as will regularly spraying the leaves with a water jet in the summer, as this dislodges the larvae, which will then be eaten by fish.

Propagation: Plants can be bought from garden centres and nurseries. Existing plants can be lifted and divided every two or three years.

Water Lily – Yellow   *Nuphar lutea*

Like the white water lily (*Nymphaea alba*), this is a rhizomatous plant, growing in lakes, ponds or rivers. A similar species, also native, is the least water lily, which is like a small version of the yellow water lily, its flowers just 4cm (1.5in) across and its leaves 10cm (4in) long. The leaves of the yellow water lily are up to 25cm (10in) long, oval in shape, rather than the round ones of the white water lily. The bright, buttercup-yellow goblet flowers, up to 7.5cm (3in) across, are displayed from June until the end of August.

Height: Above water, about 10cm (4in), in flower: below water, up to 3m (9ft). Spread: up to 1m (3ft).

Habitat: Ponds, lakes and slow-moving rivers and canals, usually in sun though it can tolerate some shade.

Garden care: Although it is susceptible to the same diseases as other water lilies, such as brown spot, lotus blight and attack by water lily beetles, all of which are best treated by immediate removal of all affected leaves and disposal by burning or in the dustbin, the main point of care with this water lily is to keep it within the size limitations you have set, for it is a prolific spreader.

Propagation: Available from some nurseries and water garden centres, it can be propagated by division in spring.

Water Soldier   *Stratiotes aloides*

This free-floating plant, related to the frogbit (*Hydrocharis morsus-ranae*), though it looks entirely different until it flowers, looks like a pineapple head that has been dropped into the water. The stiff, sword-shaped leaves radiate upwards and outwards, up to 35cm (14in) long with sharp teeth along the margins. There are separate male and female plants. The flowers when seen – which is rare – are about 5cm (2in) across, white with a yellow centre and have three petals. Sitting low in the water, they grow from the centre of the plant from May to August.

Height: Up to 25cm (10in) above the water, similar below.

Habitat: Sheltered standing water.

Garden care: This semi-evergreen needs little care once introduced, beyond occasional thinning out if it likes its situation sufficiently to spread. Generally grown for its structural impact rather than its flowers, which are not commonly seen.

Propagation: Plants are available from nurseries and water garden centres. If existing plants are happy, they will reproduce by budding from spreading stems. The buds can be separated in summer.

Water Plantain   *Alisma plantago-aquatica*

Large, very open-branched panicles of tiny white three-petalled flowers decorate this rhizomatous perennial between June and September, the flowers opening only in the afternoons. The flowering stem can be anything up to 1m (3ft) tall and is leafless. The leaves, broad ovals pointed at both ends, grow on separate stalks from the base of the plant and have prominent parallel veins. Up to 20cm (8in) long themselves, they have stalks up to 30cm (12in) long. The flowers can occasionally be pale lilac or pink.

Height: Up to 1m (3ft) in flower.

Habitat: Shallow water at the edges of ponds, rivers, lakes and canals.

Garden care: Plant in a water-garden planting basket so the plants can be lifted out easily for cutting back the leaves at the end of the growing season and for dividing plants every two years or so.

Propagation: Plants are available from nurseries and garden centres. Existing plants in the garden can be lifted and divided every two or three years. Seed can be saved and sown in wet compost or soil in pots in late summer.

Yellow Flag

Iris pseudacorus

The bright-green, sword-shaped leaves of this handsome plant can be seen decorating the edges of ponds, rivers and canals from Scotland to North Africa. It is one of two irises native to British shores, the other being the stinking iris (*I. foetidisima*), which has short-lived purple flowers in summer, developing into bright-red berries in autumn. Both are grown in gardens; the stinking iris mainly for its vivid fruits, which are held late into the winter, while the yellow flag is grown for its spectacular flowers, which open one at a time up the stem between early May and late August. Stinking iris is restricted in the wild to areas of South Wales and southern England and can grow in dry, exposed conditions as well as the more usual wetland haunts. The yellow flag, on the other hand, is widespread, but restricted to the shallows and banks of our waterways. There it can produce substantial stands, spreading by means of thick horizontal stems or rhizomes which throw up leaves and flowering stalks at regular intervals. These plants are well worth having in a garden pond or marshy area.

Height: Up to 1m (3ft), the flowers often standing up higher than the leaves.

Habitat: Fens, reed-beds, pool-sides and river banks, also flood plains and wet meadows, usually in sun.

Garden care: Do not use a rich planting mixture when planting anything in a pond. Pond plant compost is made up of mostly clay and is best confined in hessian with gravel on the top. Irises will need lifting and splitting every couple of years to confine clumps to a manageable size. A rust disease can attack these plants. If caught early, simply removing affected leaves and destroying them will get rid of the disease. Spraying anything in a pond should be avoided if at all possible. If the infection is bad, remove the plant from the pond and install in a bucket for the duration of a more severe treatment. Any insect attack on pond plants is best washed off with a water spray: then fish and pond insects will eat the offenders.

Propagation: Available at garden centres and nurseries generally. Plants can be lifted and divided every couple of years and the divisions repotted to form new plants.

POND PLANTS

	HEIGHT	FLOWERING SEASON	FLOWER COLOUR
Amphibious Bistort	10cm	June–Sept	Pink
Arrowhead	1m	June–Aug	White
Arum – Bog	30cm	May–Aug	White
Bladderwort	30cm	June–Aug	Yellow
Bogbean	30cm	May–June	White
Bur-reed – Branched	1.2m	June–Aug	Yellow
Forget-me-not – Water	15cm	May–Sept	Blue
Fringed Water Lily	5cm	June–Aug	Yellow
Frogbit	5cm	June–Aug	White
Needle Spike Rush	30cm	May–July	Brown
Pond Sedge – Greater	1.5m	May–June	Green
Reedmace – Common	3m (9ft)	June–Aug	Brown
Reed Sweet-grass	2.1m (7ft)	June–Aug	White/pink
Rush – Flowering	1m (3ft)	June–Sept	Pink
Spearwort – Greater	1.2m (4ft)	June–Aug	Yellow
Speedwell – Water	15cm (6in)	May–Oct	Blue
Starwort	15cm (6in)	May–Sept	White
Water Cress	60cm (24in)	June–Sept	White
Water Crowfoot	60cm (24in)	April–June	White
Water Lily – White	3m (9ft)	May–Aug	White
Water Lily – Yellow	3m (9ft)	June–Aug	Yellow
Water Plantain	1m (3ft)	June–Sept	White
Water Soldier	25cm (10in)	May–Aug	White
Yellow Flag	1m (3ft)	May–Aug	Yellow

Chapter Six

❖

Hedges and Shrubs

HEDGES AND SHRUBS

To MANY people, shrubs are something that flower in spring, then sit there looking green all summer, just providing a background to the flowering plants. How wrong can they be? You can have flowers on native shrubs from January right through to July by using the right combination, and that is without even using gorse (*Ulex europaeus*), which can be seen in flower somewhere in just about every month of the year.

<u>MAY</u>

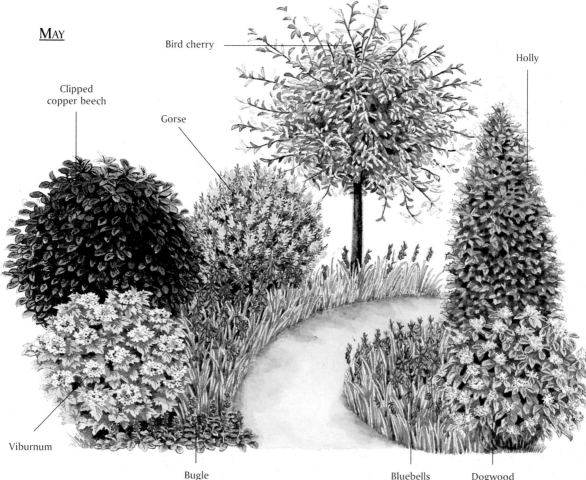

Bird cherry

Holly

Clipped copper beech

Gorse

Viburnum

Bugle

Bluebells

Dogwood

By starting with blackthorn (*Prunus spinosa*) and using hawthorn (*Crataegus monogyna*), guelder rose (*Viburnum opulus*) and wayfaring tree (*Viburnum lantana*), then adding sweet briar (*Rosa rubiginosa*) and the burnet rose (*Rosa pimpinellifolia*), you can have shrubs flowering all through late winter, spring and summer and, by the time they are over, the first of the berries have coloured up on the guelder rose and perhaps a few early ones on the holly (*Ilex aquifolium*), as well as the first hips on the wild roses. Then, as summer reaches its height in August and fades into September, the berries of the wayfaring tree and the spindle tree (*Euonymus europaeus*) come into their own. And still we have not mentioned the evergreen bushes such as box (*Buxus sempervirens*), juniper (*Juniperus communis*) and yew (*Taxus baccata*), or the late autumn and winter colour of the stems of dogwood (*Cornus sanguinea*).

So it can be seen that, even without any climbers to sprawl over or twine among them, shrubs can provide colour and interest at any time of the year, as well as helping to give the garden form and structure, especially in the colder months when the herbaceous plants are not there. Shrubs can also provide protection, as hedges, from prying eyes or invading footballs, and they are far better than fences in acting as a windbreak in exposed situations, for they filter the wind,

MAY AND JUNE

Holly

Foxgloves

Viburnum

Summer planting

Juniper

Grasses or ferns

Box

Berberis

rather than blocking it and causing uncomfortable eddies, then eventually being flattened by a particularly harsh storm and crushing the plants that they were put there to protect. Of course, hedges take up more space in a garden than do fences, which can be an important consideration in a small space, but the variety and interest given in return is more than a fair trade-off against a couple of feet of border space.

Whether you are growing a hedge, adding a few shrubs to a border to give it structure and winter interest, or doing the same for a rockery or scree bed with some of the dwarf shrubs, there is a wide choice among the forty-odd species that are native to Britain. Some of them are hard to find, either in the wild or for sale in the nurseries, but almost all are worth the search – not that the search is anything of a hardship, in itself. Half the fun of gardening is seeing what is available and tracking it down. And half the fun of choosing your plants is first going somewhere to see them growing, either naturally or in gardens. Like anything else in life, gardening needs to be enjoyed in order to be done well and the shrubs provide part of that enjoyment, both for the eyes and for the taste buds, with the likes of crab apple jelly, elderflower or elderberry wine and cranberry juice, among others, all being produced from native shrubs. And don't forget gin, which is flavoured with the berries of the juniper.

DWARF SHRUBS, JUNE

Broom

Copper beech

Box

Mezereon

Juniper

Rockrose

Cross-leaved heath

Cranberry

Purple bell-heather

White rockrose

Heather

Dogwood

Bearberry

Barberry

Berberis vulgaris

The barberry was a common hedgerow shrub until it was discovered to harbour black rust, a disease of wheat. It was then torn up wherever it was found, especially in arable areas, and is now rare in the wild. However, its highly decorative appearance has made it a prized garden plant since the earliest days of gardening in Britain. The native barberry is not evergreen, unlike some of the introduced species, such as Darwin's barberry (*B. Darwinii*) with its tiny holly-like leaves and blue berries. It has smooth, bluish bark and thorns arranged in threes on the stems, usually in the axils of the leaves. These are distinctly toothed around the margins and borne in tufts of three to five along the stem, having no stalks. They turn a rich, orangy red in autumn, when the long, oval berries also ripen to scarlet. These are not liked by birds, so stay on the bush all winter. The flowers, in April or May, may be yellow or orange. They are held in small clusters, arising from the leaf axils, and clothe the bush in a blaze of colour for several weeks. There are a number of garden cultivars, including a copper-leaved one 'Atropurpurea' which is very attractive.

Height: Up to 3m (9ft), though it can be clipped to keep it smaller.

Habitat: A plant of hedgerows and scrubland, preferring dry conditions.

Garden care: Water in well when planting. Clip lightly when necessary to save affecting the flowering of the shrub. If any rust disease is noticed, trim it out and burn the affected material or dispose of it in the dustbin. This, however, is not common.

Propagation: Available from nurseries and garden centres. Can also be propagated from seed, planting the berries when ripe and allowing them to overwinter outside. Cuttings can be taken in summer or autumn and planted direct in the garden or else in pots of coarse compost.

Blackthorn

Prunus spinosa

This bush or occasionally small tree is also known as the sloe. Its dark blue-black fruits, which are too bitter to be edible when raw, are used for making wine and flavouring gin as well as for making a preserve sometimes called sloe cheese. The dark, thorny twigs form a dense tangle of growth which is almost impenetrable by anything but insects and the smallest birds: this is probably why small birds often nest in the bush. The blackthorn bears white blossoms with prominent red-tipped stamens on bare twigs, starting in February and carrying on well into April. A hedge made up of this plant along with hawthorn (*Crataegus monogyna*) and wayfaring tree (*Viburnum lantana*) will have white blossom from early on in February to mid or late May. The blackthorn has sharp, spiny tips to its shoots as well as spines growing from the sides of them. Its elliptical leaves are small and dark green, hairy underneath and very finely toothed around the margins. They grow in small clusters, alternately on the stems, emerging after flowering has finished. The fruits have a dull, whitish bloom to their surface which reveals a shiny skin when it is rubbed off. This and the wild plum or bullace (*Prunus domestica*) are thought to be the parents of the domestic plum.

Height: Up to 4.2m (14ft), though it can be pruned to whatever size is required.

Habitat: Woodland edges and scrubland, also hedgerows. Not as tolerant of waterlogged soil as some other native shrubs.

Garden care: Firm in well when planting. Prune to size or a little smaller in autumn. Pruning can be done at other times of the year, but flowers and/or fruit will be sacrificed. Blackthorn is a relative of the plums, apples and pears and so is susceptible to many of the diseases which affect them. Red spider mite can attack the leaves, sucking the sap from them so that they turn greyish yellow and curl up, falling prematurely. Once at this stage, the infestation is probably too much for anything other than spraying with a proprietary insecticide. It is best to choose one that is as specific as possible in order to leave unharmed the more beneficial insects in the garden. Brown rot and silver leaf are two fungal diseases that can affect sloes. Affected parts should be removed and destroyed as soon as possible and if the disease persists a fungicide will be necessary.

Propagation: Plants are available from nurseries and some garden centres. There are several decorative sloe cultivars bred specifically for garden use, including the purple-leafed variety 'Purpurea', the double-flowered 'Plena' and the pink-flowered 'Rosea', as well as the wild type. All are best bought in the cold months and planted promptly. Cuttings can be taken from existing plants and rooted in a corner of the garden to be lifted and moved as soon as growth indicates rooting has occurred.

Box

Buxus sempervirens

This neat evergreen with its small, rounded, shiny leaves of dark green is rarely seen in the wild any more. It will grow into a small tree if allowed to do so, but is best known as a hedging shrub or as a subject of topiary – it is clipped into all kinds of strange ornamental shapes. Naturally rounded in shape, box copes with this well. It flowers in May, the flowers being without petals: they are just bunches of yellow stamens and green female anthers in the leaf axils near the tips of the yellowish-green stems. It will not flower if clipped, though. The bark is reddish brown when young, turning grey as the plant ages. There are numerous garden cultivars of differing sizes and densities, some with variegated leaves.

Height: A wild, unclipped tree can reach 10m (30ft) in the shade of a deep forest, but out on the chalk downs where it thrives half this size is more usual. As a clipped bush it can be kept to whatever size is required.

Habitat: Tolerates sun or shade – even deep shade – and normal or dry soils. Although usually found in the wild growing on chalk soil, it can tolerate neutral or even slightly acidic ground.

Garden care: Water in well when planting and mulch with organic matter in autumn. Clip when required, but be aware that this will prevent next year's flowering, if done later than mid summer.

Propagation: Freely available from most garden centres and nurseries. Semi-ripe cuttings can be taken in the warmer months and rooted in the ground or in pots of coarse compost.

Broom

Cytisus scoparius

A glorious mass of deep-yellow flowers clothes this native of dry heath and sandy scrub in May and June. A branched and woody shrub, it has many upright green stems with relatively few and small leaves of a rich, dark green. These are three-lobed on the older stems, but simple mid-veined ovals on the younger growth. The flowers are pea-like and about 2cm (0.75in) long, densely clothing the outer stems. There are many cultivated forms, some dwarfed for use in small gardens, others with different coloured flowers, ranging from white to deep orangy-red. There are also large-flowered varieties and some with bi-coloured flowers.

Height: Up to 2m (6ft), except for cultivars of the Warminster Broom (*C. praecox*), which grows to 1m (3ft).

Habitat: Moors, scrub and woodland edges, usually on poor soil and in full sun. Avoids lime or chalky soils.

Garden care: Flowers best on poor, sandy soil. Water in well when planting, but watering should not be needed thereafter. Prune after flowering, but do not cut into older wood. Can be prone to blackfly in summer. These can be washed off if caught early or sprayed with one of the modern insecticides that kill aphids without harming other insects.

Propagation: Available from practically all garden centres and many nurseries in one form or another. Half-ripe cuttings can be taken in summer and potted in a gritty compost, where they should root by late autumn.

Butcher's Broom   *Ruscus aculeatus*

Named for its use in ancient times, this evergreen shrub grows in shady woods in southern England and Wales and is found more often by touch than by sight, especially in the summer, for the tips of its stiff, diamond-shaped leaves are sharply pointed. The whole plant is a rich, dark green in colour, the leaves glossy like those of holly (*Ilex aquifolium*). One of the unusual points about this plant, though, is the fact that these leaves are not leaves at all but broadly flattened stems, the leaves being tiny, little more than scales in the junctions of these stems. This explains the other remarkable

thing about butcher's broom, which is that the flowers are borne singly in the centre of the 'leaves', generally on the underside. They appear in February and March and though tiny – barely 0.75cm (0.25in) across – are exquisitely formed. Lying flat to the mid-rib of the stem segment, each flower has six narrow white outer petals surrounding a purple corolla tube with creamy-white stamens at its centre. They are followed in autumn by prominent round red berries, about 1cm (0.3in) across. Altogether an unusual and fascinating little shrub for a shady spot in the garden.

Height: Up to 1m (3ft). Width similar.

Habitat: Shady woods and damp hedge bottoms.

Garden care: Water in well when planting and ensure that it does not dry out too much in summer. In the unlikely event of attack by rust fungus, remove and destroy affected parts.

Propagation: Available from some nurseries. Cuttings can be taken in late summer or autumn and potted in compost outside. They should be planted out before the winter cold really sets in.

Dog Rose

Rosa canina

Wild roses generally have single flowers, as opposed to the blowsy double confections of the cultivated varieties, most of which originate in China. The dog rose can have pink or white flowers with a small, loose boss of yellow stamens in the centre and a faint, if pleasant, perfume. Usually found in hedgerows, where it grows up to 3.3m (10ft) through the other shrubs, the dog rose's stems few and widely separated, it provides the root stock for many grafted garden roses. The suckers on these, if left to grow, will be found to be the dog rose. Due to its loose habit and need for some support from surrounding shrubs, the dog rose is often thought of as a climber, whereas the only true climbing British rose is the inappropriately named field rose (*R. arvensis*). The field rose has creamy-white flowers in July and August, while the dog rose flowers from late May to July. The hips of the field rose are much smaller than those of the dog rose. The advantage that the field rose has over the other wild roses is that it will tolerate some shade.

Height: Up to 3.3m (10ft); field rose up to 2m (6ft).

Habitat: Hedges and woods, preferring a sunny position, though the field rose will tolerate shade.

Garden care: The dog rose can be grown as a free-standing shrub, when it will be shorter and its stems more plentiful, but still slightly arching. However, it really prefers the support of close association with other shrubs. The field rose can be grown over a pergola or arch or through other shrubs. Both are excellent if combined with spring-flowering shrubs such as blackthorn or barberry. All roses can be susceptible to fungal diseases such as mildew and black spot, though the native ones less so than the garden varieties. These can be treated with fungicides or the affected leaves picked off and disposed of in the dustbin or burnt. Aphids and whitefly can also be a problem, but if caught early can be knocked off with a spray of water. Otherwise there are insecticides that do not harm the beneficial insects, or a soft soap spray can be used.

Propagation: Some of the wild roses are available from specialist wildflower or rose nurseries. Once you have a stock, hardwood cuttings can be taken and heeled in to root over winter with a bed of sand in the bottom of the hole. By spring they should be rooted and ready to transplant to the required position.

Dogwood
Cornus sanguinea

This is a native shrub that has made the move very successfully into our gardens, where it is grown primarily for the autumn and winter colour of its stems. There are a number of varieties available through nurseries and garden centres, varying in stem colour from yellow through orange and brown to red, some with green leaves, others with a strong silver variegation. All look very good throughout the year, with the narrowly oval, pointed leaves appearing in April, followed a few weeks later by flat panicles of white flowers in May and June. These develop into black berries, each on its own upright stalk, which contrast well with the rich red-brown of the autumn leaves, before they fall and leave the coloured stems to brighten a sunny winter's day.

Height: Up to 3.3m (10ft), if allowed to mature.

Habitat: Woodland and shady hedgerows, though it can tolerate a sunny aspect. Will grow in wet or dry soil, but prefers neutral or alkaline conditions.

Garden care: Water in well when planting and firm the roots in. Clip the bush back every year for the first three or four years to encourage bushiness, then coppice every three years to keep the stems young and their colour bright.

Propagation: Readily available from garden centres and nurseries. Semi-ripe cuttings can be taken in spring or summer while the plant is in growth, or hardwood cuttings in autumn. Each should be planted up immediately and left until top growth indicates rooting has occurred. In the case of hardwood cuttings, this will not be until the following spring.

Elder
Sambucus nigra

One of our more common hedgerow shrubs, the elder is nevertheless often used in the garden: it grows quickly, and bears good flowers and useful fruit. People have long used the frothy-white flowers, borne in broad, flattened heads up to 15cm (6in) across in June and July, for making cordials and sparkling wine as well as for eating fried with pancakes. Likewise, the black autumn berries, though toxic when raw, are used to make wine or jam. The elder has hollow, pith-filled stems which break easily and can be made into whistles or pea-shooters. The bark is a pale grey-green in colour; the bark of the main trunk is thick, ridged and corky. The young stems are soft and green. The leaves, larger and darker than those of the ash (*Fraxinus excelsior*), are divided into definite toothed leaflets, usually two or three opposite pairs and a terminal one. They have an unpleasant, rank smell, unlike the flowers, which smell sweet and fruity. There are several garden cultivars, such as the golden-leaved elder (*S. n.* 'Aurea') and a number of dark-leaved forms, including the new 'Black Beauty': this has pink flowers, burgundy leaves and grows just 30cm (12in) a year, so is easily kept in control in the smaller garden.

Height: The elder can grow into a small tree if conditions allow, but is more usually found as a shrub around 2.1m (7ft) high.

Habitat: Woods and hedgerows. Tolerates wet or dry soil, as long as it is rich in nitrogen. Can tolerate shade, but prefers sun.

Garden care: Water in well when planting and if the leaves show signs of drooping thereafter. Elder can be coppiced every three years, if necessary in a confined space. Contact with elder can cause itching in some people, so gloves are a wise precaution when handling the plant.

Propagation: Plants are available from nurseries and some garden centres. Berries can be sown in pots outdoors in autumn to germinate in the following spring.

Gorse
Ulex europaeus

Gorse is one of those plants that is essential to a gardener seeking to establish a long season of interest, for although its main flush of flowers comes between February and the end of April, it is well known that you can find a sprig of flowering gorse somewhere at literally any time of the year. Gorse's numerous spines and dense growth make it an excellent hedging plant. And if planted in a closely packed or shaded site, it can achieve a height of over 2.7m (8ft), though more usually it grows to between 1–2m (3–6ft). Though naturally a rather irregular shape, it can be clipped in late summer or autumn to about 15cm (6in) smaller than you want it and it will grow in and flower on the new shoots. A smaller variety called 'Flore pleno' is available, which has double flowers and grows to just 1m (3ft) or so. The long trusses of bright-yellow flowers, interspersed with spines, are beautifully fragrant and provide a lovely contrast to the dark-green foliage or the vivid blue of a summer sky. The foliage of a mature plant consists entirely of spines. It is only when the plant is young that it has normal leaves, which are trifoliate in the manner of a clover. Also known as furze and whin in different parts of the country, the gorse has short, pea-like pods which split with a loud cracking noise in autumn to release very shiny olive-green, pea-like seed. There are two similar species. Dwarf gorse (*U. minor*) is a smaller plant, with shorter spines and deeper-yellow flowers, and western gorse (*U. gallii*) is very similar but tends to flower later, its main flush being in late summer and autumn. Probably the best gorse hedge, therefore, is mixed common gorse and western gorse.

Height: Up to 2.7m (8ft), unless 'Flore Pleno' or dwarf gorse are used, which grow to only about 1m (3ft).

Habitat: Heaths, roadsides, banks and woodland clearings. Not on calcareous, or limy, soils.

Garden care: Dead-heading will extend flowering even more than usual. If the plant is to be clipped into shape, then this should be done in early autumn, to allow time for regrowth before new flowers are formed. Can take fairly severe pruning if necessary, but this is best kept to a minimum if possible.

Propagation: Both common and western gorse are available from nurseries throughout the country. 'Flore Pleno' is sometimes seen in the larger garden centres. Once plants are established seed can be collected in autumn and sown either fresh or in spring. Like all the pea family, the seed needs to be scarified before sowing.

Guelder Rose

Viburnum opulus

Its large, palmate leaves with three or five pointed lobes can lead to confusion, especially in spring, between this and the wild service tree (*Sorbus torminalis*) or one of the maples. Unlike these, the guelder rose is a bush not a tree, and the leaves are broader than those of the wild service tree and more toothed than those of most maples. The main difference becomes apparent in May and June, when the guelder rose comes into flower. In its wild form – previously known as swamp elder after its broad, flattened bunches of red berries – it bears flattened heads of white flowers, the inner ones tiny and numerous, the outer ring large, five-petalled and sterile. The whole head is around 7.5cm (3in) across, like a small hydrangea flower head, and they are borne prolifically over the surface of the bush. The name guelder rose correctly refers only to one form of the bush – the one most commonly used in gardens – which was discovered growing as a wild sport in Holland in the sixteenth century. This bears globular heads of flowers of the type normally around the edges of the rosette and is therefore sterile. It is commonly known as the snowball tree. The berries of the guelder rose, bright red in colour, are oval in shape, unlike the round, usually black, ones of the elder (*Sambucus nigra*). They are beginning to ripen by mid-summer and contrast well with the dull loganberry red of the leaves in autumn. The berries show up even better after the leaves have been shed, but unlike the berries of the elder they are poisonous.

Height: Up to 4m (12ft), but more usually 2m (6ft).

Habitat: Commonly found in hedgerows and still popular for the purpose, it is naturally found in damp areas including marshes and fens as well as in clearings in oak woods.

Garden care: Pruning to maintain shape and size can be done in late summer, after flowering. Clearing up leaves after they have fallen is always a good idea, as it prevents the continuance of diseases into the following year and removes at least one hiding place for snails and slugs.

Propagation: The snowball tree, being sterile, can only be propagated by taking cuttings, semi-ripe in late summer or hardwood in autumn, or by layering. This is a method in which a branch is selected and bent down to touch the ground, where it is pegged into place; usually the underside of the point of contact with the ground is cut part way through, if possible, just before a bud. This point will then root and the new plant can be cut away from the parent and moved to a new site. Similar methods can be used with the guelder rose, but in this case the berries can also be used. Like most berries, they need to be stratified (given a period of cold) to encourage germination. This can be achieved by planting them in a pot of coarse compost and leaving it outside over winter. The seed should then germinate in spring. Otherwise, plants of either variety and several other cultivars are available.

Hawthorn

Crataegus monogyna

One of the earliest of the native shrubs to come into leaf in the spring: the early leaves are a fresh-green colour, unlike those later in the season after flowering, which tend to be reddish. The leaves are roughly triangular in overall shape, but variously lobed, having anything from three to seven lobes. They are a little over 2.5cm (1in) long. The flowers come in May, in dense clusters along the branches, giving the plant its other name of May blossom. Hawthorn naturally forms a dense, thorny bush and can be used for agricultural hedging and, with careful clipping, for a garden hedge, forming a dense, neat growth. The autumn berries can be made into a sweet jelly. Left on the plant, however, they form a decorative red covering through autumn and well into winter, providing a food source for a variety of songbirds. Midland hawthorn (*C. laevigata*) is similar, except that it tends to form a small tree rather than a bush. It is more shade tolerant than the common variety and so is sometimes found in woods. It has a red-flowered variety 'Rosea pleno flore' and a variety of garden cultivars, some of which are crosses with the common hawthorn. There are white, pink and red-flowered varieties, some double-flowered, others single. All these different varieties of hawthorn make lovely ornamental trees.

Height: Up to 13m (45ft), if allowed, but commonly 1.5m (5ft) in hedge or garden use.

Habitat: Commonly found in hedgerows and open grassland, also moorland and marshes.

Garden care: Pruning is best done after flowering, as with many shrubs, but that, of course, precludes the formation of the berries. If these are required, pruning can be done in winter or early spring, before the leaves come out. Flowering will be reduced, but not entirely eliminated.

Propagation: Pot-grown or bare-rooted plants are available from garden centres and nurseries. Cuttings are easily rooted. Hardwood cuttings should be taken with a heel, trimmed of excessive leaf and planted, preferably in a fairly free-draining soil, in summer or early autumn. Growing from seed is a more laborious method. The berries need to be picked in early autumn and stored in damp sand for eighteen months before they will sprout. They can then be planted up individually to grow into small bushes before being put out.

Hazel

Corylus avellana

This useful shrub bears its catkins throughout the winter, after the leaves have fallen. They appear in September or October and remain about 2cm (0.75in) long until February, when they spring into growth, reaching about 5cm (2in). Borne at or near the ends of the branches in bunches of twos and threes, they are golden in colour and dance in the breeze. Near to them on the stem are the tiny red star-like female flowers. Flowering is over by mid-April and the leaves are then becoming prominent, growing alternately from the reddish-brown stems. They are broadly oval, with toothed edges and characteristic lop-sided bases. They turn a rich, warm yellow in autumn as the female flowers ripen into large round brown nuts, born on long stems in bunches of two or three. These are the cobnuts enjoyed by many at Christmas. The plant can be coppiced and the pliable stems used for a variety of purposes. Hazel is very tolerant of pruning.

Height: Up to 4.5m (15ft).

Habitat: Hedgerows and oak and beech forests, where it forms a dense understory to the bigger trees. Tolerant of sun or shade, damp or dry soils.

Garden care: Firm in well and water thoroughly when planting. Prune to required size in summer, though you will lose that year's crop of nuts.

Propagation: Plants available from nurseries and a few garden centres. Hardwood cuttings can be taken in late summer and heeled into the ground to root.

Heather

Calluna vulgaris

Otherwise known as ling, this largest of our seven native species of heather bears long spikes of pinkish-purple flowers from June or July right through September. It can be distinguished from its relatives by its tiny leaves, overlapping each other and set tight to the stems in groups of four. Also, its flowers tend to be on one side of the stem. If allowed to age, the plant becomes very woody and loses its freshness, but hard clipping after flowering each year can prevent this. In the wild this is accomplished by grazing and by regular managed burning of heathland, but in the garden shears can achieve the same end result. Heather flowers later than most shrubs and can help to give a suitable garden form and shape.

Height: Up to 1m (3ft).

Habitat: Heath and moorland, also pinewoods. Needs neutral to acid soil. Sun or light shade.

Garden care: Make sure that you have a suitable soil, on the acid side of neutral, before considering these plants. If you have, they are not fussy about moisture content, though the related Bell Heather (*Erica cinerea*) prefers drier soil and Cross-leaved Heather (*E. tetralix*) prefers wetter ground. Clip back hard, though not into old wood, in autumn after flowering is finished.

Propagation: One of the more widely available native plants, heather can be bought as plants from garden centres, nurseries, market stalls and a variety of other outlets, more commonly in autumn, along with several of its close relatives. Non-flowering shoots can be taken as semi-ripe cuttings in the warmer months and potted in sharp-drained compost to root in a few weeks. A 50:50 mixture of potting compost and sharp sand works well, watered thoroughly before inserting the cuttings around the edge of the pot and sealing inside a plastic bag to await the beginning of new, bright-green growth to signal the success of the cuttings, which can then be potted up individually.

Holly

Ilex aquifolium

Found in almost every home at Christmas, holly can grow into a fair-sized tree in the wild if allowed to, but is generally found as a shrub. This is almost invariably the way it is grown in our gardens. There are too many cultivated varieties to mention. Some have white variegated leaves, some golden variegated. Some have yellow or orange berries instead of the natural red. Some have even been bred without the characteristic deeply indented, multi-pointed edges. But the natural wild plant is as decorative as any. Its deep-green, waxy leaves clothe it thickly all through the year. They have roughly eight to twelve spine-like points arranged around their stiff edges and grow alternately from the dark-brown stems. The main trunk is green when young, maturing to grey and remaining smooth. Holly has small white flowers, held close to the stems, in May. On female bushes, these ripen to bright-red berries by autumn, providing winter food for the birds as well as decorative garlands for our doors and hearths.

Height: Can grow to as much as 18m (60ft), but can be clipped and shaped to whatever size is required.

Habitat: Happy in full sun or in the shade of a forest, the one thing that holly is not keen on is wet ground.

Garden care: Water in well and provide a low stake when planting the young shrub. Clip to size in August or September. Otherwise little care is needed by this tough and adaptable evergreen.

Propagation: Available from garden centres, nurseries, market stalls and DIY centres. Berries can be planted, but will need a cold spell over winter before they germinate, which can take eighteen months. Cuttings can be taken and rooted in the garden in the warmer months.

Juniper – Common

Juniper communis

This very variable shrub is one of two species – the other being the Chinese juniper (*J. chinensis*) – which are commonly grown in our gardens. One of Britain's three native conifers, the juniper can grow into a conical tree up to 6m (20ft) or as a low shrub with horizontally spreading branches. A little like the yew (*Taxus baccata*), the leaves, or spines, of the juniper are short and sharply tipped, held out from the stem and often in threes. The flowers are carried in the axils of the spines towards the tips of the stems, but are difficult to see. The berries, forming in late summer, are carried through the winter with a similar colour to the spines, but then ripen in the second year to a deep, bluish black. It is these that give gin its distinctive flavour. There are numerous garden cultivars, including the tall, pencil-thin 'Hibernica' and the low, spreading, yellowish 'Depressa Aurea'.

Height: Up to 6m (20ft), depending on conditions and variety. More usually, 30cm–3.3m (1–10ft).

Habitat: In the wild, juniper is an upland plant, growing on moorland and downs. It can thrive in dry or moist conditions, in sun or semi-shade.

Garden care: One of the advantages of plants like juniper and the heathers, which made them so popular in the late 1960s and 1970s, was the lack of care that they needed. Like any plant they should be watered in well when planting, and it is worth keeping a watch on them for the first few weeks just to see that they establish well, but after that no care should be needed apart from lightly clipping if the plant gets too large for its site.

Propagation: Available from garden centres, nurseries and other plant sales outlets. Cuttings can be taken in summer and rooted in pots of coarse compost.

Mezereon

Daphne mezereum

Rare in the wild, this upright, little-branched deciduous shrub is often grown in gardens for its sweetly scented, rich-pink flowers, which appear from February to April when there are still few, if any, leaves on the plant. Most of the long, tongue-like, dark-green leaves appear after the flowers are over. They are up to 12cm (5in) long, with a strong central rib, wider towards the pointed tip than near the base in the same way as those of the horse chestnut (*Aesculus hippocastanum*).

There is a large tuft of leaves at the apex of the plant and groups of three or more down the stem and on the few branches. The small, red berries appear in late summer and autumn. They are poisonous to humans, though not to birds. The strong fragrance and bright-pink colour of the flowers make the mezereon a welcome plant in the garden in early spring. There is also a white-flowered form called 'Alba' for those borders where a rich pink just will not do.

Height: Up to 1m (3ft).

Habitat: Deciduous woodland, usually on chalk or limestone soil. The plant prefers at least partial shade and does not need a lot of water.

Garden care: Daphnes have a reputation as being difficult plants to grow, but this is one of the least problematic, being one of the two that are naturally at home in Britain. Once planted – at which point it needs watering in well – the mezereon should be disturbed as little as possible. Being a small shrub with upright stems, pruning should not be necessary. It must be recognized, however, that it is not the longest-living shrub around and may need replacing after four or five years. This is not because it does not like your garden, but because it has run its natural course.

Propagation: Plants are available from garden centres and from nurseries. They are a little expensive, but it is worth shopping around as they are not easy to propagate for yourself. You could try a hardwood cutting in late summer, with sand in the base of the trench, but do not be too disappointed if it does not work.

Periwinkle

Vinca sp.

Two species of Periwinkle grow wild in Britain, the greater periwinkle (*V. major*) which has flowers up to 5cm (2in) across and the lesser periwinkle (*V. minor*) which has flowers half the size. The former grows throughout lowland Britain, the latter just in the south of England. The greater periwinkle is probably an introduction from Europe. In both cases, the evergreen leaves are pointed, smooth and leathery, the stems lax and trailing. The blue flowers open in spring and occasionally through the summer from pointed buds in which the petals are twisted clockwise. There are variegated cultivars grown for garden use as well as the natural type with mid-green leaves. Either will root readily wherever the stem touches the ground, including in water.

Height: Up to 75cm (30in), though they spread up to twice that.

Habitat: A very adaptable plant, naturally found in hedges and woodland edges, the periwinkle can grow happily in wet or dry soil, in sun or shade.

Garden care: Water in well when planting and prune in summer to maintain the required size and spread.

Propagation: Available from garden centres, nurseries and other plant outlets, the periwinkles are easily rooted by layering – pegging down a stem on to the ground, where it will root and can then be cut away from the parent plant.

Privet – Wild

Ligustrum vulgare

Primprint or prim, as it was called in earlier times, was used in gardens until the middle of the nineteenth century, when its close relative Oval-leaved privet (*L. ovalifolium*) was introduced from Japan and found to be more reliably evergreen than the native plant, which only keeps its leaves through mild winters. The leaves are larger and longer than those of the introduced species, set in pairs along the twigs and shiny in appearance. They are often curled upwards along the edges and are mid or dark green. The privet flowers profusely, the tiny, sickly-smelling white flowers borne in small conical spikes up to 5cm (2in) long during May and early June. The flowers are followed by a heavy crop of pea-sized berries which are purple when young, ripening to almost black and staying on the bush through the winter.

Height: Up to 4.5m (15ft), though it can be clipped to any size below that.

Habitat: Generally found in hedgerows, it will also be found on waste ground, though rarely north of the Midlands. It tolerates dry conditions well, but becomes sparse and lanky in shade and is more inclined to drop its leaves in polluted areas such as cities.

Garden care: Water in well when planting. If rust appears on the leaves, clip off and destroy the affected stems. Clip after flowering, preferably to a size a little smaller than you want, so that it can grow in again without affecting next year's flowering. If you find the scent of the flowers unpleasant, then clip again in autumn to discourage them.

Propagation: Available from nurseries. Cuttings can be taken in the warmer months and rooted in the garden or in pots of compost. The berries can be picked and planted in pots outside, where they should germinate for the following spring.

Rose – Burnet

Rosa pimpinellifolia

It is claimed that over a hundred species of wild rose grow in the British Isles, but only five of these are commonly found and only four of those are available commercially. These can be split into pink ones and white ones. The commonest of the white ones are the burnet rose and the inaptly named field rose (*R. arvensis*), which is the only true climbing rose native to Britain and is found in woodland and shady places. It bears bunches of white flowers in June and July, followed by bright-red hips in autumn. The burnet rose forms a dense, spiny

bush anything from 15cm (6in) to 1.2m (4ft) in height. It gets its name from its leaves, which are like those of the salad burnet. From May through to July it is covered in showy, cream-white blooms with the typical central boss of yellow stamens. These are followed by glossy purplish-black hips in late summer and autumn, which are spherical and about 2cm (0.75in) across, looking quite spectacular in the late summer sun. Its neat, dense habit makes the burnet rose a good choice as a hedging rose.

Height: Up to 1.2m (4ft) though often smaller.

Habitat: Open, sunny situations, preferably on light, even sandy, soil. Can tolerate wind and even salt spray, so is happy growing wild on sand dunes.

Garden care: Give this rose the conditions it grows wild in – hot and dry – and it will thrive. However, it can also be grown in the Midlands on clay. Just dig in coarse grit underneath it and give it a generous planting hole and it should do well. Like all roses, it can be susceptible to black spot and mildew as well as aphid attack.

As always, the best defence is to give the plant the conditions it enjoys, so that it will grow healthily and strongly and be able to fight off minor infestations on its own. If this does not work sprays are available for rose diseases. Infected material can be picked off and aphids can be washed off with a spray of soapy water.

Propagation: Plants are available from nurseries. Hardwood cuttings can be taken in autumn and heeled in over winter in a slit trench with some sand in the bottom, where they should have rooted by spring.

Sea Purslane

Halimione portulacoides

This spreading shrub has silvery-grey leaves and soft stems, growing from low, twisted woody main stems. It is much branched and has deep, searching roots to anchor itself at the tide-line, the lower stems re-rooting where they touch the ground. The flowers are pale yellow and tiny, borne in clusters at the tips of the stems from July to September. An ideal subject for the rockery, where it makes a fine background to contrasting plants that have pink, purple or blue flowers.

Height: 30–60cm (12–24in).

Habitat: Naturally found in salt marshes, usually on the banks of tidal creeks where it will grow on mud or rocks. Thrives in full sun and in dry or salty conditions.

Garden care: This tough plant can take all the heat and aridity our summers can throw at it, but it will not abide water logging in fresh water and it will need some protection from very hard frosts, as evidenced by the fact that it does not grow naturally in Scotland except for in the far south-west.

Propagation: Available from some nurseries, it can be lifted and divided every three years or so. Stems can be pegged into the ground to root then cut away to form new plants, or semi-ripe cuttings can be taken in summer and rooted in gritty compost.

Spindle Tree

Euonymus europaea

Despite its name, the spindle rarely attains the dimensions of a tree, usually being found as a medium to large shrub. Its smooth bark is greenish when young, maturing to grey; the branches are somewhat four-winged, as are the fruit and the flowers. The leaves are borne in opposite pairs. They are light-green, thin and pointed, their edges finely serrated. In autumn they turn a rich, dark red, contrasting well with the pink four-lobed fruit. The bush flowers in May or June, the flowers having four narrow, white petals with four yellow-tipped stamens and a green ovary at the centre. These are born in loose clusters on the somewhat sparse branches, giving the whole bush a light, airy feel which is belied by the toughness of its wood, from which it got its name. The wood is pale, dense and very hard, and was used in former times to make spindles for the hand-spinning of wool before the spinning wheel was invented. It was also used for making pegs and skewers and now produces high-quality artist's charcoal. Several highly decorative varieties have been bred over the years for garden and park use.

Height: Up to 6m (20ft).

Habitat: Hedgerows, woodland edges and scrubby slopes, particularly on chalk and limestone.

Garden care: A low stake provided when planting will help to get the roots established, as will watering in well. Despite its delicate good looks, this shrub is relatively trouble-free, having a natural in-built insecticide (which was once used to drive lice away from school children).

Propagation: Plants are available from nurseries and some garden centres. Bare-root specimens should be planted in winter, whereas pot-grown ones can be planted any time, as long as sufficient watering is done to establish good root growth afterwards. Cuttings can be taken with a heel in late summer and potted to stand in a sheltered spot and root over winter, or the seed can be harvested and sown in pots outside.

Spurge – Wood

Euphorbia amygdaloides

A member of a truly worldwide genus of plants, the wood spurge shares these islands with three other spurges, all small annual weeds of various situations. There are several varieties of wood spurge grown for garden use, including a purple-leaved one and a red-stemmed one, among others. Actually a small shrub, the natural form has brownish-orange young stems and dark-green leaves that are long, slender and stalkless, growing in fives or sixes around the stems. The showy bracts are a pale, yellowy green, sometimes edged with red, and contain usually three tiny flowers. Each set of bracts looks like a flower itself and is borne on its own short stalk, growing from the leaf axils, generally at or near the top of the plant. If cut or wounded, the spurges exude a milky sap which is irritant, if not toxic, to most people, but the plants are still popular in gardens, where the showy bracts give a good display for several months through spring and early summer, and the evergreen nature of the leaves and stems gives form to the shade garden through the winter.

Height: Up to 75cm (30in), eventually.

Habitat: Deciduous woodland, especially on chalk or limestone soils.

Garden care: Water in well when planting, as with any other plant. Cut flower heads away when they have finished if seed is not required, but wear gloves when handling this plant, as the sap is a strong irritant. It must be kept away from the eyes and you should wash your hands after handling the plant, just in case.

Propagation: Seed and plants are available from nurseries and garden centres. Seed can be saved from existing plants and sown fresh in the garden or in pots left outside over winter.

Sweet Briar

Rosa rubiginosa

Also known as the apple-scented rose for the scent given off by the brownish glands on the undersides of its leaves when they are crushed or even when they are just wind-blown on a hot, sultry summer's day. This is one of the pink-flowered varieties of wild rose that are native to these islands. The flowers are similar in size to those of the dog rose (*R. canina*), but a darker pink with less prominent stamens. The leaves are paler and the hips more orangy in colour and round in shape, with hairs over their surface. The sweet briar flowers in June and July and forms a denser bushy growth than the dog rose, so is better for hedging or as a specimen bush in a mixed border.

Height: Up to 3m (9ft) if competition for light is strong, but more usually about 2m (6ft).

Habitat: Hedgerows, waste ground and scrub. Can tolerate most soil conditions, but prefers a heavier soil to too much sand. Generally found in southern England and the Midlands.

Garden care: Like all roses, a good feed with well-rotted organic matter when planting will do it good, as will a mulch with the same material every autumn. Most roses do not like the soil to dry out too much, and this one is no exception. Any sign of aphid or fungal attack should be treated as soon as possible to retain strength in the young shoots and therefore flowering vigour. Dead-heading will prolong the flowering season, but of course will reduce the number of hips carried into the winter. Like many of the wild species roses the sweet briar is thorny, so gloves are advisable when handling the plant.

Propagation: Plants are available from some nurseries. Hips can be potted up in the autumn and left outside over the winter to germinate. Cuttings can be taken in spring or autumn and heeled into a trench with some sand in the bottom. These should root in a couple of months.

Tutsan

Hypericum androsaenum

Unlike the other native members of the hypericum family – the various St John's worts – this shade-loving plant is actually a shrub, in common with several of the introduced species which are widely used in our gardens. Tutsan has the characteristic bright-yellow blooms with their prominent spray of stamens in the middle, though the flowers are no more than 2.5cm (1in) across and borne in bunches of three to five at the tips of the shoots. Apart from the smaller size of its flowers, this resinous-smelling bush can be distinguished by the large, prominent, shiny-yellow ovary at the centre of each flower. After fertilization, this becomes a fruit which turns from yellow to red, along with the petals, which then fall away leaving the fruit to ripen to black. The leaves are large and oval, those towards the tips of the shoots having a reddish tinge to them. Overall, this small shrub has a soft kind of attractiveness that works well in most gardens.

Height: Up to 1m (3ft).

Habitat: Commonly found in damp woods and hedge bottoms, it grows well in shade and can thrive in wet or dry soils.

Garden care: Water in well when planting. Trim to size if necessary in autumn, after the fruit has set. Once established in your garden it will seed itself around freely. When seedlings are large enough to be handled they can be transplanted or potted up and given to friends. Tutsan takes well to town life and can stand salt air; it is found growing healthily near the coast as well as inland.

Propagation: Plants and seed are available from specialist nurseries. Soft cuttings can be taken in the warmer months and rooted in pots of damp compost, or the ripe fruits can be harvested and sown in pots to overwinter outside.

Wayfaring Tree   *Viburnum lantana*

The common name of this shrub is a corruption of the name given to it in the sixteenth century by the botanist John Gerard, who called it the wayfarer's tree because he found it to be so abundant along the old drove roads of southern England. Before that it was called the hoarwithy, for its downy white hairs on the undersides of its leaves and the willow-like suppleness of its stems. Unlike the other native viburnum, the guelder rose, this bush has thick, rounded leaves, evenly toothed along the margins and about 5cm (2in) long. They are borne in opposite pairs along the stem. The flowers are borne in broad, slightly domed panicles, 6cm (2.5in) across and spread generously over the bush in April and May. The berries are slim and oval, starting off green and maturing through the late summer and autumn from red to shiny black. It is a dense, neat bush ideal for hedging, and can stand any amount of pruning or even laying, as has been done for centuries to field hedges. In these, the stems of the hedge plants are cut part-way through just a few centimetres up from the base and bent over, then tied into place to form a dense, even hedge.

Height: Up to 4.5m (15ft).

Habitat: Field hedges, woodland edges and scrubland, usually on chalk or limestone, though it will happily grow on clay or loam. It is not found naturally further north than Yorkshire.

Garden care: This resilient shrub needs little in the way of help from people, as it is ideally adapted for life in our climate. Pruning to size and shape can be done in late summer, when any diseased, dead or crossing branches can be removed for the sake of appearance. The plant can occasionally be attacked by black spot if it is stressed. This can be treated with a fungicide spray or the affected leaves simply removed and disposed of in the dustbin or by burning.

Propagation: Plants are available from nurseries, though rarely in garden centres. Semi-ripe cuttings can be taken in late summer or hardwood cuttings in autumn. The seed, if used, needs to be stratified or given a period of cold before germination.

Wormwood

Artemesia absinthum

The Latin specific name gives away the primary use of this silver-leaved shrub as the flavouring for vermouth and absinthe. Having twisted, woody main stems, wormwood's main growth is much-branched and soft, with both stems and leaves silver in colour and silky to the touch. The leaves are much-divided and exceedingly soft. It bears yellow flowers in July and August, but is mainly grown for its foliage. Probably the best variety is 'Powys Castle', which has fine, lacy leaves and makes a good, robust plant. Wormwood is very attractive in bright sunshine and is also surprisingly tolerant of shade, despite its being a silver-leaved plant. Much smaller, but equally appealing and sometimes available for use in the rockery is the sea wormwood (*A. maritima*), which is just like a tiny version of the above, growing to just 30cm (12in) or so tall. Both these plants are essential for the sensory garden, where touch is so important.

Height: Up to 1m (3ft).

Habitat: Waste ground and dry slopes, usually in sun but tolerant of shade.

Garden care: The one thing to note about the wormwoods is that they are easily starved and if this happens the lower foliage will die away, leaving a straggly brown plant with silvery tips. This can easily be avoided, by not leaving them in pots too long and by mulching with well-rotted manure or compost in the autumn.

Propagation: Available from nurseries and some garden centres. Soft cuttings can be taken in the warmer months and rooted in pots of coarse compost. Seed can be saved and sown in pots outside in autumn or spring.

HEDGES AND SHRUBS

	HEIGHT	FLOWERING SEASON	FLOWER COLOUR
Barberry	3m (10ft)	April–May	Yellow/orange
Blackthorn	4.2m (14ft)	Feb–May	White
Box	10m (30ft)	May	Yellow
Broom	2m (6ft)	May–June	Yellow
Butcher's Broom	1m (3ft)	Feb–March	White
Dog Rose	3m (10ft)	May–July	Pink
Dogwood	3m (10ft)	May–June	White
Elder	2.1m (7ft)	June–July	White
Gorse	2.7m (8ft)	Jan–Dec	Yellow
Guelder Rose	4m (12ft)	May–June	White
Hawthorn	13m (45ft)	May	White
Hazel	4m (12ft)	Feb	Yellow
Heather	1m (3ft)	June–Sept	Pink/purple
Holly	18m (60ft)	May	White
Juniper – Common	6m (20ft)	April–May	White
Mezereon	1m (3ft)	Feb–April	Pink
Periwinkle	75cm (30in)	April–July	Blue
Privet – Wild	5m (15ft)	May–June	White
Rose – Burnet	1.2m (4ft)	June–July	White
Sea Purslane	60cm (24in)	July–Sept	Yellow
Spindle Tree	6m (20ft)	May–June	White
Spurge – Wood	75cm (30in)	April–June	Yellow
Sweet Briar	3m (10ft)	June–July	Pink
Tutsan	1m (3ft)	June–Aug	Yellow
Wayfaring Tree	5m (15ft)	April–May	White
Wormwood	1m (3ft)	July–Aug	Yellow

Chapter Seven

Shade Plants

SHADE PLANTS

SOME WOULD SAY that we seem to have more shade-loving plants in Britain than any other group. That may well be true, but it is hardly surprising when you consider that, before the interference of people, most of the British Isles was covered in forest of one sort or another. Many of those so-called shade-loving plants are no such thing. They are simply shade-tolerant and enjoy full sun as much as any of the meadow species, if they find an opportunity to grow in such conditions. Violets, periwinkles, the foxglove (*Digitalis purpurea*), the bluebell

(*Hyacinthoides non-scripta*) and bugle (*Ajuga reptans*) as well as daffodils and the ramson (*Allium ursinum*) will all grow as well in full sun as they do in shade. Others, such as the primrose (*Primula vulgaris*), lungwort (*Pulmonaria officinalis*) and wood anemone (*Anemone nemerosa*) grow better and more strongly in shade than they do in a sunny site.

There is no need for deep shade in order to grow these plants. The sun can touch them for part of the day, as long as they have some shelter from it for much of the time. Growing such plants at the bases of walls, fences and shrubs is ideal, as well as under trees or at the base of a trellis. These are the plants that will brighten that dark, uninviting spot in the garden or grow lushly in a border where the sun-lovers become lanky and straggly for lack of light. They are the ones that make your sheltered, quiet spot in the shade into a green haven instead of a dark hole. And although most of the well-known shade plants are spring-flowering, there are plenty which go beyond that all-too-brief season, giving colour and form from January or February right through to September. In late winter the process begins with snowdrop (*Galanthus nivalis*), which continues through the main spring flush into summer with plants such as the foxglove, which can be seen in flower as late as mid to late August, and the

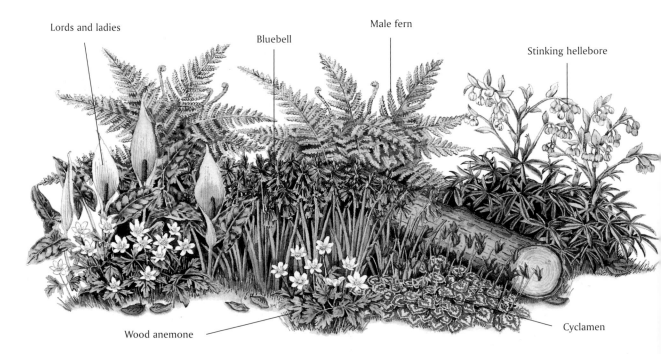

Lords and ladies

Bluebell

Male fern

Stinking hellebore

Wood anemone

Cyclamen

MAY

132

wood cranesbill (*Geranium sylvaticum*), among others. We move into autumn with bugle and herb robert (*Geranium robertianum*), both of which start flowering in spring and carry on pretty well right through, as well as the native cyclamen (*Hederifolium purpurescens*), which flowers from June to September. Then, through late autumn and the depths of winter, interest can be maintained with the evergreen, sometimes variegated leaves of the periwinkles, wood spurge (*Euphorbia amygdaloides*), some of the ferns and grasses and the strange, prickly shrub butcher's broom (*Ruscus aculeatus*).

So, shade in the garden is not something to be avoided or worried about, but something to be enjoyed as a pleasant haven. As long as you pick your plants according to the situations they need to fill as well as according to your own tastes, there is nothing to worry about and plenty to enjoy.

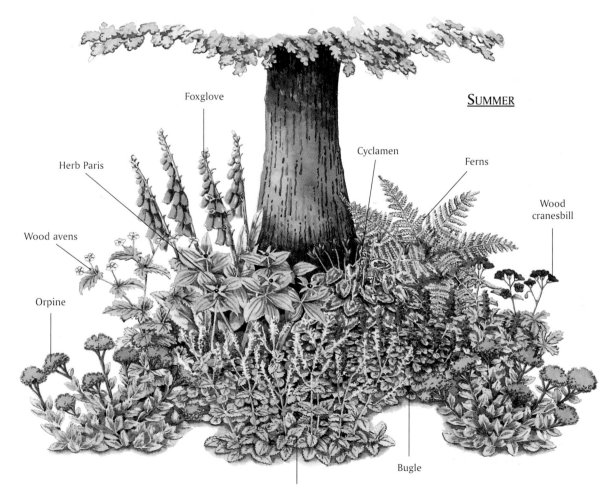

Foxglove

SUMMER

Herb Paris

Cyclamen

Ferns

Wood cranesbill

Wood avens

Orpine

Bugle

Woodsage

Anemone – Wood   *Anemone nemerosa*

Also known as the wind flower, the leaves of this common plant are divided into three coarsely toothed lobes, which are sometimes deeply split. There are three stem leaves, their stalks arising from near the top of the slender, upright stem, a short distance below the single large flower. The flowers have six narrow petals around a central boss of yellow anthers. They can be up to 4.5cm (1.75in) across and are open from March into May. Later, basal leaves arise singly on long, slim stalks from the narrow rhizome. There are several cultivated varieties of this lovely plant, with flowers of pink or blue, including 'Robertsoniana' and 'Alleni', both of which are blue.

Height: Up to 20cm (8in).

Habitat: Mainly found in deciduous woodland, but also in damp, shady meadows, often on alkaline soils.

Garden care: Best planted 'in the green' – that is, in the growing stage rather than when dormant. Like Snowdrop (*Galanthus nivalis*) and Winter Aconite (*Eranthis hyemalis*), they establish much more readily this way. Watering will be welcomed in a dry season, and a mulch with well-rotted organic matter will do the plants good as well.

Propagation: Plants and seed are available from nurseries and some garden centres. Existing plants can be lifted and divided every three or four years, in early summer. Seed can be saved and sown in pots left outside over winter.

Bluebell   *Hyacinthoides non-scripta*

The garden variety of this bulbous plant is usually the closely related Spanish bluebell or a hybrid of the two. These are preferred because of their more even distribution of flowers around the stem, but are often less vigorous than the native, which can also sometimes be found in pink or white variant forms. These colour variants are rare in comparison to the usual rich-blue, bell-shaped flowers hanging in umbels of anything from four to sixteen, on a stem that droops under their weight. Growing from the base of the plant are six to ten 28cm (11in) long, strap-like leaves, which last a good six weeks after the flowers fade towards the end of May.

Height: Up to 45cm (18in).

Habitat: Deciduous woodland.

Garden care: Like many plants, these are shade-tolerant rather than shade-lovers, though the brilliance of their colour is best appreciated on a dull day in the shade. They like rich soil, but are tolerant of most sites and will self-seed widely if allowed. Rust can be a problem, but usually not until the leaves are beginning to die back anyway, so this should be taken as a sign that it is time to clear the foliage, taking care not to put it in the compost heap and so perpetuate the disease. A light mulch with compost or chipped bark in autumn is welcomed, but not essential.

Propagation: Bulbs can be bought from the garden centre or nursery. Seed needs to be sown in autumn or kept in a cold place for several weeks before sowing.

Daffodil

Narcissus pseudonarcissus

What garden could be complete without the bright spring presence of the daffodil to brighten the short days of February and March? The original wild variety, still seen in some areas of Wales and the West Country in woods and damp meadows, has scented, deep-yellow flowers with a wavy edge to the 5cm (2in) central trumpet and blue-green stems and foliage. Now, however, there are an incredible number of different varieties on the market. You can have daffodils in flower from January well into June, leaf colours from blue-green to yellowish and flower colours from white through cream to yellow and even pink, some with petals the same colour as the trumpet, some with contrasting colours. There are daffodils only 10cm (4in) high and plants over 60cm (24in) tall, some with single flowers and some with several on a stem. And all from just a handful of original species including our own native wild daffodil.

Height: Up to 35cm (14in).

Habitat: Woods and meadows. Likes humus-rich soil; acid-tolerant and moisture tolerant.

Garden care: Plant bulbs so that there is about 5–7.5cm (2–3in) of soil above their noses, either in the border or in a meadow setting. Keep leaves on the plant for at least six weeks after flowering finishes in March or April. If space is needed before then, dig up and re-plant in an unused area of the garden until leaves begin to go brown. Bulbs can be left in all year or dug up in summer and re-planted in late autumn for next year's display. Feed with powdered fertilizer rather than manure after flowering. If clumps are too large and overcrowded or begin to come up 'blind', i.e. without flowering, lift and divide in summer.

Propagation: Bulbs or plants can be bought in garden centres and nurseries in late summer or in flower in spring. Plant in autumn. Lift and divide clumps in late summer.

Enchanter's Nightshade

Circaea lutetiana

Despite its name, this delicate-looking perennial is not a relative of the deadly nightshade (*Atropa belladonna*) or the woody nightshade (*Solanum dulcamara*), but is related instead to the willowherbs. Its dark, slender stems carry pairs of long-stalked, pointed oval leaves around 10cm (4in) long. Above these, the stems branch to become flower spikes bearing loose, dainty spikes of white or sometimes pink flowers. The flowers are tiny with two deeply divided petals behind a pair of long-stalked anthers and an almost equally long-stalked stigma. Unlike many plants of shady places, this is not a spring flowerer, but displays its delicate and tiny flowers in late summer, when the branches are full of leaves and the shade of the forest floor is at its deepest.

Height: Up to 60cm (24in), but often closer to 40cm (16in).

Habitat: Shady hedge bottoms and woodland floors, in damp or dry conditions.

Garden care: This plant grows up each year from an underground rhizome that is not easy to eradicate once established, so is best confined by some physical means into the required area, at least until you are sure that you are happy with it. Water in dry weather, if grown in a dry or densely planted position. Cut down to the base in late autumn. Dead-head to extend flowering season and prevent seeding.

Propagation: Available as plants or seed from some specialist nurseries. The seed heads, with their covering of hooked hairs, can be saved and sown in pots of compost in late summer or early autumn, then left outside to germinate in the spring. Clumps can be lifted and divided every three years.

Fern – Hart's Tongue

Phyllitis scolopendrium

Unique among the native ferns, this one does not have the much-divided fronds classically associated with that group of plants. Instead it has smooth, shiny, strap-like fronds up to 5cm (2in) wide, which unfurl in the spring up to 30cm (12in) long to make a handsome clump that looks good almost all through the year. Naturally a woodland plant, it provides an excellent textural contrast to the more usually shaped ferns and looks wonderful with dappled sunlight shining through its pale green fronds from behind. As with most ferns, the hart's tongue enjoys moisture and high humidity, but along with several others it will grow in a drier situation, such as the top of an old wall, as long as it has some shade in compensation. Its closest relatives are the spleenworts and it is sometimes listed as *Asplenium scolopendrium* in accordance with this relationship. The spleenworts are generally ferns of drier situations.

Height: Up to 30cm (1ft).

Habitat: Damp, shady places. Wet woodland. Also drier situations such as on old walls, though still shade tolerant. Looks better for longer if shaded.

Garden care: Water well after planting, like most plants, but keep this one moist until it is well established. Old leaves can be cut away after new ones begin to appear in spring. Unlike the hostas, this plant does not appear to suffer greatly from slug or snail damage, so a sharp grit mulch should not be necessary.

Propagation: Plants are widely available from general outlets. Like all ferns, these propagate themselves by spores found on the back of the fronds in autumn. These are normally dispersed by the wind, but can be given a helping hand onto a pot of moist compost, which should then be sealed into a polythene bag to retain moisture. Patience must be applied liberally while nature takes its course; small ferns are eventually formed in the following spring.

Fern – Male
Dryopteris felix-mas

The fern used as the typical example of its group in biology classes across the country, the male fern's name has nothing to do with its gender, but was a means of identifying it from the quite similar lady fern, which is more finely divided, delicate and 'feminine' in appearance. Both have the typical fern structure: several leaves arising from a central point, each one divided into leaflets along its main stalk, each of those leaflets divided again along its own central rib, the whole thing shaped so that it widens gradually from the base to about two-thirds of the way along, then tapers sharply back to a pointed tip. The male fern is one of our larger ferns, its tall shuttlecocks of leaves, darker on the upper surface than underneath and quite upright in mid to late spring when young. Later in the year, the fern's spores form dark-brown lines along the undersides of the central ribs of the leaflets.

Height: Up to 1.5m (5ft).

Habitat: Woodland, shady ditches and hedgerows. Sometimes among stream-side boulders.

Garden care: Choose a site with some shade and preferably dampness. Soil does not have to be deep, but needs to be moisture-retentive. Remove old leaves after new ones have grown in late spring.

Propagation: Ferns propagate by means of spores, developed and carried on the undersides of the leaves. When these become ripe, a few leaflets can be picked and pegged down, right-side-up, on to pots of moist compost. If the pots are left in a cool, damp place, then germination should take place and young ferns will form in the following year. Ferns are currently enjoying a resurgence in their popularity as garden plants and are commonly available in garden centres and nurseries.

Forget-me-not – Wood

Myosotis sylvatica

By far the prettier of our two dry-land species of forget-me-not, the other being the common variety (*M. arvensis*), which is a tall, slender plant with tiny pale-blue flowers and a tendency to suffer from grey mould. The wood forget-me-not is a bushy mid-green plant, hairy, with elliptical leaves which are stalkless and carried alternately on the branching stems. At and near the top of the plant are loose bunches of sky-blue flowers, with bright-yellow centres. Flowering is from April or May to July. This lovely little plant combines wonderfully with a range of different flowers in the garden, such as the tulips, wallflowers or primulas. Very popular in the garden, along with the smaller introduced species *M. alpestris*, of which there are also numerous varieties.

Height: Up to 35cm (14in).

Habitat: Open woodland, on damp or dry soils. Can tolerate neutral or alkaline soils. Prefers at least some shade.

Garden care: These easy-to-grow plants require little care, except for watering in hot weather and a little dead-heading. Replace the plants each year.

Propagation: Best grown as a biennial, plants and seed are readily available in nurseries and garden centres. Seed can be saved from plants in the garden. It should be sown in pots or trays in summer, ready for planting out in autumn or early spring.

Foxglove

Digitalis purpurea

One of the cottage garden classics, this tall, stately plant is tolerant of a wide range of conditions, from damp woods to sun-drenched stone walls. There are dozens of different species and garden varieties of foxglove, from white, through yellow and cream to pinks and purples, and 30cm–1.5m (12in–5ft) in height. In recent times, the garden varieties have become much more densely flowered and showy, but the basic native purple foxglove still has a charm all of its own. The tubular flowers, often with spotted markings inside the lower lip, are borne in one to three columns, generally up one side of the tall flowering stem from late May through to August. The greyish-green felty leaves form a rosette close to the ground in the first year, then send up a single stem in the second year, the lower portion of which has leaves smaller than those of the rosette below a long spike of flowers. The plant will seed copiously, but if allowed to do so it will then die, as all biennials do. If, however, the flower spike is removed as soon as the flowers fade, it will live on to flower another year. In this way, plants can be kept for up to three or four years.

Height: Up to 1.5m (5ft), though some varieties are shorter.

Habitat: Generally thought of as a plant of woodlands, but also found growing wild on rocky scree and even on stone walls. Happy in sun or shade, but the garden hybrids especially do like some dampness.

Garden care: If you are growing garden hybrids, water in dry weather. If growing the native plant, then water if it begins to droop. Otherwise, foxgloves are tough and hardy plants: most soils and situations will do, though they grow especially well if given a reasonably rich soil and some shade.

Propagation: Seed and plants are widely available from nurseries, garden centres and market stalls, especially in spring. Seed, whether bought or saved from your own plants, should be sown in spring or early summer and planted out where they are to flower in autumn, when they are 5cm (2in) high or more.

Herb Robert

Geranium robertianum

One of our prettier wild flowers, this annual geranium has dark-green or more usually red stems and bright-green leaves, finely divided to give an almost ferny effect, topped by bright-pink buds. It flowers from May right through to December, if the weather is sufficiently mild. The whole plant is covered with fine, short, silvery hairs which are displayed admirably when the light is behind them. It is a very widespread plant, being distributed almost all over the northern hemisphere, probably because it is so adaptable in its choice of home. It is equally at home in sun or shade, in moist or dry conditions, its fairly lax stems growing through and around other plants to achieve their maximum height. If no support is available it will stay small and compact, be it in sun or shade. It looks lovely on the rockery in combination with thrift or on the shaded back of a stone wall, along with maidenhair spleenwort. Alternatively, it can brighten up a shady woodland site after the bluebells have finished their display, either on its own or combined with bugle or stitchwort.

Height: Up to 50cm (20in).

Habitat: Woods, grassland, walls and seashore. Usually but not always on neutral to limy soil. Herb Robert grows well in either sunny or shady conditions.

Garden care: Very little can go wrong with this most adaptable plant, once it is established. Sow seeds in autumn or spring, where the plants are required and water in well, or plant individual plants in spring. Remove faded flower clusters, especially if you do not want seed to set.

Propagation: Seed is available from specialist nurseries. Otherwise, you would be an unusual gardener if you did not have this plant arrive of its own accord, if it is not there already. Seed can be saved in a paper bag from the narrow, pointed seed capsules that follow the flowers. Treat as an annual, sowing seed in autumn or spring in pots or trays of compost. Seed should be scarified before sowing to aid germination. Plants sown in this way or ones that have self-set in the wrong place in the garden can be transplanted in spring to their required positions.

Lily-of-the-valley   *Convallaria majalis*

Sweet-scented white bellflowers adorn this rhizomatous plant in long umbels through April and May if it is given a site in which it is happy. A single stem rises from the ground with a pair of broad, tongue-shaped leaves, from between which the flower stem rises. The flowers droop from one side of this on short, fine stalks. It is found naturally in woodland on lime-rich or sandy soils, where it can find that special combination of rich soil with good drainage. A tough little plant, it will grow on most soils, though it is far happier in shade, even against a north-facing wall. Under a window on such a wall, you would get the fragrance wafted richly into the room on a damp evening. Combines well with the bluebell, as both like shade and are strong spreaders. There are a few garden cultivars: one large-flowered variety, a pink-flowered variety and even a couple of variegated varieties, 'Albostriata' and 'Vic Pawlowski's Gold'.

Height: Up to 30cm (12in).

Habitat: Woodland, usually on lime-rich or sandy soil, also churchyards and north-facing hedge banks.

Garden care: Once established in the garden, the only jobs are to tidy up the dead flower heads and to control its spread, which is by underground stems, or rhizomes. It can be chopped back with a spade in autumn to the required size and the 'cuttings' either discarded, placed in other sites around the garden and watered in, or potted up and given to friends or relatives.

Propagation: Plants are readily available from garden centres, nurseries and so on. Best planted between October and March. Cuttings can be taken in the form of a chunk of the plant, as described above, or more precisely as root cuttings, laid shallowly in trays of compost in autumn or early spring.

Lords and Ladies   *Arum maculatum*

Also called cuckoo pint, this common perennial grows from a large tuber deep in the ground. It has arrow-shaped leaves, each on an individual stalk from the base, as is the flower – or more correctly, flower spike. This appears in April and May, taking the form of a purplish spike, surrounded by a yellow-green spathe like a monk's cowl, open at one side and forming an elegant flute-shaped bowl at the base, in which are the reproductive parts. Later, in mid to late summer, this is replaced by a tight bunch of brilliant red berries, each about the size of a pea and very toxic if eaten.

Height: Up to 50cm (20in).

Habitat: Woods and shady wetlands, often on alkaline soils, preferring rich soil with plenty of organic matter.

Garden care: Water in well when planting and ensure it does not dry out in summer. Mulch with well-rotted garden compost or manure in autumn or spring and cut down any dead stems in autumn.

Propagation: Plants and seed are available from specialist nurseries. Berries can be planted in pots of compost, sealed in plastic bags to prevent drying out and left outside over winter. Crowns can be lifted and divided in early spring every 3 years.

Lungwort

Pulmonaria officinalis

This old garden favourite was named for its white-spotted leaves, which reminded people of lungs. Some of the leaves are small and clasp the stems of this softly hairy plant, while others are large, open, broad and pointed elliptical in shape, and up to 20cm (8in) long. The flowers are borne in panicles, some nodding, some upright. They open from red buds into sky-blue flowers, each 2.5cm (1in) or so long and tubular, the open face a little more than 0.5cm (0.2in) across. The plant is semi-evergreen, the leaves dying back in summer or autumn only to reappear after a few weeks and perhaps be held all through the winter, depending on the weather. The flowers appear early in April and last well through May and sometimes into early June. There are several cultivars sold in garden centres, many from foreign species, but our own native is as good as any and can be found in a white-flowered form as well as several different blues. Narrow-leaved lungwort (*P. longifolia*) is another native, though only in southern England. It has longer, slimmer leaves, often without spots.

Height: 30cm (12in).

Habitat: Shady places, especially on heavy soils.

Garden care: Water in well when planting and if the soil dries out in summer. Dead-head for tidiness, rather than to prolong flowering significantly. Remove dead leaves when they decide it is time for a rest. Lift and divide plants every three years or so, as they will spread substantially in ideal conditions.

Propagation: Plants available from nurseries, garden centres and market stalls in spring. Existing plants can be lifted and divided every two or three years, the divisions replanted promptly and watered in well.

Pendulous Sedge

Carex pendula

The leaves of this rhizomatous evergreen perennial are 30–100cm (12–36in) long and up to 2cm (0.75in) across, coming from reddish brown sheaths. The flower spikes, on stems that are often around 1m (3ft) tall, are long and slender. There is an orangy-red male spike at the top of the stem and from three to five yellow-flowered female spikes below it. The spikes are held one above the next along the stem, drooping away from the stem as their weight pulls it over to give the plant its characteristic stance and hence its name. The flowers are carried through May and June, the tiny fruits in place of the female flowers until August. Pendulous sedge is the largest of our native sedges apart from those growing in water and makes a bold and decorative garden plant, making clumps up to 60cm (24in) across.

Height: Up to 1.5m (5ft) in flower, though often only two-thirds of this height.

Habitat: Damp woods and shady stream banks, often on clay soil.

Garden care: Water in well when planting and ensure the ground does not dry out in summer.

Propagation: Plants and seed available from some nurseries. Lift and divide clumps every three years. Seed can be sown in late summer in pots for planting out in spring.

Pimpernel – Yellow *Lysimachia nemorum*

More closely related to creeping Jenny (*L. nummularia*) and yellow loosestrife (*L. vulgaris*) than to the scarlet and bog pimpernels (*Anagalis arvensis* and *A. tenella*), this pretty little plant is much more delicate in appearance than creeping Jenny, though it is another low, creeping perennial. The flowers, carried from May through to September, are up to 2cm (0.75in) across, bright yellow and star-shaped, with five petals. The light-green leaves are 4cm (1.5in) long, of a rounded triangular shape with very short stalks, arising from lax, thin stems which creep among other plants or across the forest floor. The flowers are on long, slim stalks. A bright, attractive plant for a shady area of the garden in summer.

Height: 6cm (2.5in), but spreads up to 30cm (12in).

Habitat: Woodland and shady hedges, often on limestone soils, though it will thrive in pine forests. Can tolerate damp or dry soils.

Garden care: Water in well when planting and again if the soil dries out too much in summer. Dead-head regularly to ensure a continuous supply of flowers and cut back dead stems in winter.

Propagation: Plants and seed are available from specialist nurseries. Seed can be saved from existing plants. Best sown fresh in late summer or autumn, in pots left outside.

Poppy – Welsh *Meconopsis cambrica*

As can be seen from the Latin name as well as from the flower itself, this plant of Wales, the West Country and the Lake District is more closely related to the blue poppies of the Himalayas than to the true poppies of the English lowlands. Another plant that is often confused with the Welsh poppy is the yellow horned poppy (*Glaucium flavum*) which inhabits coastal areas of Britain and Europe, just above the tide line. Though this has flowers of equal size and beauty to those of the Welsh poppy, it is distinguishable by the long, sickle-shaped fruits and by its sadly short life, growing as a biennial or at best a short-lived perennial. The Welsh poppy, on the other hand, is longer lived, has more poppy-like seed heads and is much less demanding in its requirements. Indeed, it will grow just about anywhere, in damp or dry conditions, in sun or shade. It can be seen clinging to life in the shady side of a dry-stone wall or giving a splash of brilliant colour in the middle of a sunny border, where it mixes well with geraniums or campanulas or provides a bright accent in a bed of lady's mantle (*Alchemilla mollis*). The flowers are yellow or orange and naturally single, though there are double varieties available as well as red ones from some sources. They are about 5cm (2in) across, born singly on 30cm (12in) stems above a clump of attractive light green feathery foliage from May until September, though the main flush is in early summer.

Height: 35cm (14in).

Habitat: Usually dry or shady places, often on lime-rich soils. A good subject for the shady side of a rockery or the middle of a mixed border.

Garden care: Water in well when planting, adding peat or compost to the soil. If planting in the sun, do not allow the soil to dry out too much in the summer. Dead-head regularly to prolong flowering.

Propagation: Seed and plants are available from a wide range of nurseries and garden centres. Various forms available. Seed can be sown in pots outside in late summer or early autumn.

Primrose

Primula vulgaris

Once one of Britain's most common and best-known wild flowers, the primrose has suffered greatly in the wild from people digging it up to take back home. Sadly, this practice was often a waste, because insufficient root was dug up with the plants and they died. However, it is thankfully far less commonly done nowadays and indeed is unnecessary because the variously coloured varieties sold commercially will often revert to the natural state after a couple of years anyway. If anyone needs a description of this endlessly popular plant, it has long, crinkled, tongue-like leaves in a rosette which is generally flat to the ground. These are up to 20cm (8in) long, pale green, paler underneath, the undersides having a light covering of very fine hairs. The flowers are borne singly from February to May on downy stalks from the centre of the leaf rosette, opening to 4cm (1.5in) wide, butter yellow with a darker-yellow centre. The primrose flowers have five petals, each split at the tip, and deep-set central reproductive parts, some with the stamens prominent, others with the female style more obvious. There are numerous commercially grown varieties of primrose, and the plant is available in many different colours, ranging from white to rich reds and blues, some with the central dark yellow eye, some without. Also, several double-flowered varieties of primrose have been bred for garden use.

Height: Flowers up to 15cm (6in) high.

Habitat: Woodland, hedge bottoms and short-cut pasture. Often in shade, which seems to promote stronger growth. Usually on heavy or limy soils.

Garden care: Water in well when planting. Dead-head regularly to prolong flowering. If not allowed to set seed, plants will regroup and flower again later in the summer. They can be in flower as early as Christmas and kept going on and off until August.

Propagation: Plants are available from just about anywhere you can think of to buy them. Seed from garden centres and nurseries. Existing plants can be allowed to self-seed, then the young plants dug up and moved to the desired position, or seed can be saved and sown in pots or trays outside in summer. The seed needs a period of cold before it will germinate, so be patient if sowing in pots and do not keep them in the greenhouse.

Ramsons

Allium ursinum

A member of the onion family, along with the decorative alliums often used in gardens, this strongly aromatic bulbous perennial is also called wild garlic and has been used for the same purposes as that plant, which is also a close relative. Ramsons usually grows in large colonies in the wild, so that the strong smell will be noticed sometimes before the starry white flowers in spring and early summer. The leaves are long-stalked and broadly strap-like, similar to those of lily-of-the-valley (*Convallaria majalis*); the flowers are borne in spherical bunches on long stalks separate to those of the leaves. Looks lovely with bluebell (*Hyacinthoides non-scripta*) and red campion (*Silene dioica*).

Height: 15–35cm (6–14in).

Habitat: Deciduous woodland and hedge bottoms, often on damp ground.

Garden care: Although it looks pretty, it does not smell so and is better at the far end of the garden, especially if there is an area there which is frequented by unwelcome visitors, such as the neighbour's cat. Bulbs should be planted in autumn and kept watered throughout the summer, after flowering is over. Dead stems and leaves can be cut away in late summer and a mulch of well-rotted garden compost applied after this.

Propagation: Bulbs are available from some nurseries and occasionally in garden centres. Clumps can be lifted and divided every three years or so.

Snowdrop

Galanthus nivalis

Like the primrose and the bluebell, this lovely little plant is not as common as it once was in the wild, because people used to go out and dig them up for the garden before such selfish and often pointless activity was made illegal. Sadly, while the primrose and the bluebell are recovering in numbers and distribution, the same does not seem to be true of the snowdrop, for it is still quite rare in the wild. Its nodding, white bellflowers, with green tips to the inner petals, need little introduction, however. In some sheltered parts of the south-east of England, they are open in time for Christmas, though more usually it is January or February before the three outer petals and three shorter inner ones open to herald the beginning of spring.

The flowers are borne singly on slender stalks, the leaves narrow and greyish-green, up to 15cm (6in) long, rising from small, brown bulbs, just beneath the surface of the earth. There are dozens of garden cultivars, many actually bred from the closely related *G. elwesii*, from Europe. They include giant ones, double ones, dwarf ones and countless others. There is a garden in the Cotswolds that opens to the public and holds over one hundred and forty varieties.

Height: 7.5–15cm (3–6in).

Habitat: Open woods and copses, where it will enjoy sun for part of the day and shade for the rest, with plenty of organic matter to feed the bulbs.

Garden care: Plant in the green, that is with the leaves still growing. Planting dry bulbs can be unsuccessful and in any case, they take much longer to establish. Mulch in March, after the flowers have finished, with leaf mould or compost. Feeding through the summer will do no harm if an easy source is available. Dig up and transplant bulbs from overcrowded bunches in February or March, after the flowers have finished, but while the leaves are still green.

Propagation: Available from garden centres and nurseries. Will spread once established, and can be divided in spring.

Solomon's Seal   *Polygonatum multiflorum*

Unusually, this plant is named for its roots, which were said in ancient times to resemble the seal of Solomon, otherwise known as the Star of David. The roots are thick, white and tangled. The stems, on the other hand, are long and unbranched, often with several to a plant and the leaves arranged along the upper half to two-thirds in twin rows, standing out horizontally or semi-upright, each one broadly elliptical in shape. In May and June clusters of narrow, white, bell-shaped flowers, each 2cm (0.75in) long, hang beneath the stems. These develop later into blue-black berries. There are several closely related species native to Britain. The plant usually sold in garden centres is a cross between *P. multiflorum* and angular Solomon's seal (*P. odoratum*), which has an angled stem and usually solitary flowers. This species is found in more open, drier places, such as rocky outcrops, dry grassland and woodland clearings. A third species, whorled Solomon's seal (*P. verticillatum*) is found only in Scotland in the wild. This has narrower leaves and flowers than the other two, and an angled stem like *P. odoratum* but clusters of flowers like *P. multiflorum*. Also available in garden centres is (*P. japonicum* 'Variegatum'), which has white stripes on the leaves.

Height: About 60cm (24in).

Habitat: A woodland plant, it will thrive in most soil types, but benefits from having peat or compost added to the soil when planting. Thrives best in shade or partial shade.

Garden care: Mulch in autumn and again in spring, water if necessary in dry spells and keep a watch in summer for sawfly caterpillars, which can strip the leaves in a few days if left unchecked.

Propagation: Available from nurseries and garden centres. Lift and divide overcrowded clumps every three years or so, replanting the young, outer sections where they are required and watering in well.

Sorrel – Wood   *Oxalis acetosella*

There are several species of Oxalis, this being one of two that are native to Britain: the other has tiny brownish leaves and even tinier yellow flowers in summer, spreading to form a low mat of foliage between rocks and stones, often in shady areas. Generally, the non-native species are sun-lovers, their flowers pink or red and 2.5cm (1in) across. All have five petals and clover-like trifoliate leaves. Some are bulbous, some grow from rhizomes and others are annuals. The wood sorrel is a rhizomatous perennial which used to be common in woods throughout Britain, though it is less so now. It has slender, pinkish stems, leaves and flowers being borne individually on stems up to 12cm (5in) long. The delicate white flowers, up to 2.5cm (1in) across and sometimes veined lilac or purple, appear in April and May and close up at sunset. The leaves are a pale, yellowish green.

Height: Up to 12cm (5in), though often smaller.

Habitat: Woodland, often in damp places but sometimes among rocks. Thrives best in shade.

Garden care: Dig in some compost when planting, water in well; afterwards if the stems begin to droop, cut away old leaves in autumn.

Propagation: Seed and plants available from specialist nurseries. Plants can be dug up and divided in spring.

Stinking Hellebore   *Helleborus foetidus*

One of several hellebores grown in our gardens, including the Christmas rose (*H. niger*) and the lenten rose (*H. orientalis*), this one is actually a native. It has a thick, branched, pale-green stem and long-stemmed, dark-green leaves, each made up of anything from three to nine narrow strap-like leaflets, arranged in a fan-like design. These can be anything up to 15cm (6in) long, though the ones nearer the top of the plant are smaller. The flowers are borne in panicles at the tops of the stems. Each flower is up to 2.5cm (1in) across, drooping and bell-shaped or globular with purple edges to the yellow-green petals. The stinking hellebore flowers from late February to the end of April or even into May. The other native hellebore, the green hellebore (*H. viridis*), is shorter in maximum height and has wide-open green flowers. Flowering period and distribution as well as habitat are much the same for both species.

Height: Up to 75cm (30in), though often somewhat smaller.

Habitat: Dry slopes, scrub and woodland, often on lime-rich soil. Very shade-tolerant, though it can take the sun for at least part of the day.

Garden care: Water in well when planting, dead-head after flowering has finished, unless seed is required. Plants can suffer from rust disease. If this is noticed, affected leaves should be removed and destroyed.

Propagation: Plants and seed are available from nurseries and garden centres, especially in early spring. Seed can be saved from existing plants and sown in pots or allowed to self-seed in the garden. Plants can be divided every three years.

Stitchwort – Greater   *Stellaria holostea*

A pretty, delicate-looking perennial of woods and hedgerows which flowers abundantly in spring. The flowers are up to 2.5cm (1in) across, each of the five white petals being divided almost into two down the centre. Although the leaves, borne in pairs up the stem, are stiff and rough, the stem itself is not. Further up it is square and erect, but at the base it is fine and weak, so that the plant needs the support of others around it, if it is not to sprawl. However, it looks lovely combined with bluebells, meadow cranesbill or red campion, either in a small arrangement or a broad swathe. It flowers from April to June.

There are two other stitchworts native to Britain. Lesser stitchwort (*S. graminea*) is a smaller, finer plant of heath and dry grassland, with paler green stems and leaves and smaller flowers, which appear in May. Bog Stitchwort (*S. alsine*) has smaller flowers again, the green sepals between the petals being longer than the petals and open from May to July. Also similar in appearance, but difficult to obtain, is the field mousear (*Cerastium arvense*). This has rounded, hairy leaves and similar flowers to the greater stitchwort, but is lower to the ground at only 12cm (5in) high and lives on dry grassland and rocky areas.

Height: Up to 60cm (24in).

Habitat: Woodland and hedgerows. Tolerant of shade.

Garden care: Plant in groups and give the support of close association with other plants and you will get a starry white display for several weeks. Cut down the stems in late summer after seed has set, or dead-head if seeding is not required.

Propagation: Seed is available for a few specialist nurseries, but it is well worth the search. Sow shallowly in pots or trays in late summer or early autumn and leave outside to germinate, then plant out when the young plants have reached sufficient size to bear transplanting.

Violet – Common Dog *Viola riviniana*

This is the most common of the ten species that grow wild in Britain, many of which are difficult to tell apart. It is a small perennial which has a rosette of dark-green, heart-shaped leaves, usually hairless and finely toothed at the edges, about 2.5cm (1in) long on long stalks. The flowers are on even longer stalks, arising from the leaf nodes. They are scentless, violet-purple and about 2.5cm (1in) across. Often there are dark lines near the centre of the flower. The flowers have five petals. The larger central one of the three lower petals has a spur on the back, which is hollow, blunt and pale. The common dog violet flowers from early March into June. There is an early dog violet (*V. reichenbachiana*), which flowers two to three weeks earlier and has a dark spur. Also the dog

violet (*V. canina*), which has much narrower leaves and flowers and grows up to 30cm (12in) high, being found only locally but in a wide variety of habitats from sand dunes to fens. The marsh violet has very rounded leaves, is much paler in both the leaves and the flowers, and is found in wetland situations flowering in May and June. The hairy violet (*V. hirta*) has more triangular, brownish green leaves, grows to about 15cm (6in) high, flowers in April and May and, of course, is hairy. Generally, the violets are invaluable plants for spring colour in a range of varied situations. All these different violets make compact plants which die back unobtrusively in winter but re-emerge eagerly in spring to decorate a range of habitats, from damp shade to dry rocks.

Height: Up to 20cm (8in).

Habitat: Grassland and woodland floors, also among rocks. Sun or shade, but does not appreciate very acid soils or wetness.

Garden care: Very little is needed. Dead-heading will prolong flowering to some extent, but otherwise the plants can be left to their own devices once planted. They will happily self-seed around

the garden if allowed to do so, but not in an invasive manner. If clumps get too large, they can be dug up and divided.

Propagation: Plants and seed are available from nurseries. Seed can be saved from existing plants, which can also be dug up and divided every two or three years. Cuttings can be taken in summer and potted up in coarse compost to root in a few weeks.

Woodruff

Galium odoratum

Sometimes called sweet woodruff for the smell of new-mown hay which it exudes when dried, this slender perennial is a member of the bedstraw family. Its narrow, pointed leaves are up to 5cm (2in) long and are carried in whorls of six to nine around the stem. The flowers are tiny, white funnels, opening to four petals at the top, and are borne in broad bunches at the tops of long stalks during April and May. A very pretty plant when found in a clump in a spring woodland, it has a delicate look lacking in some of the other spring flowers.

Height: Up to 30cm (12in).

Habitat: A woodland plant, it is found on neutral or alkaline soils, often in beech woods where the soil is too dry for many other plants. Can tolerate deep or partial shade or some sun.

Garden care: Its delicate looks are misleading. Not much can do significant harm to this little perennial. Water it in well when planting, dead-head when the flowers are over and cut back in late autumn. A mulch with well-rotted organic matter in autumn or early spring will do it good, but is by no means essential.

Propagation: Available from specialist nurseries as seed or plants, the seed can be saved from existing plants and sown in pots outside in summer or a head of flowers can be left on the plant and allowed to self-seed.

Wood Sedge

Carex sylvatica

This densely tufted, evergreen perennial grows from short rhizomes. The soft, bright, yellowish-green leaves can be up to 60cm (2ft) long, but are more often about half that or even much less, depending on the growing conditions. It is a tolerant plant, growing in sun or shade, on damp or dry soil. The arching tufts are very decorative with or without the flowering stems, which appear from mid-May to July and can be up to 60cm (2ft) tall, thin and arching, with a group of three male flower heads at the tip and female heads born further down the stem, on long side-stems that have a leaf at their base. The decorative value of this native sedge has long been recognised and varieties of it are available in some garden centres.

Height: Anything from 10–60cm (4–24in).

Habitat: Usually found in woods, on clay or chalk, often on damp ground, it is also happy on open moorland, possibly persisting here in the wild from former forestation. It can also tolerate dry conditions but grows smaller, though just as pretty.

Garden care: Water in well when planting, preferably providing some organic matter into the planting hole. Remove dead leaves and stems as this prevents the harbouring of pests.

Propagation: Plants available from some garden centres, also seed from some nurseries. Plants can be lifted and divided every three years. Flower heads can be bent down and pegged to the ground once seed has set. Shaking the head and then giving it a light covering of compost and watering well should dislodge the seeds and begin the process of germination. Young plants can then be transplanted when large enough to handle.

Yellow Archangel *Lamiastrum galeobdolon*

Looking like a nettle, especially when not in flower, this square-stalked perennial with opposite pairs of toothed leaves, lacking the indented bases of some of its less amenable close relatives, is becoming rare in the wild. It has found favour among gardeners, especially the variegated 'Florentinum' and one or two less keenly spreading varieties such as 'Silver Carpet', both of which are available in some garden centres. This is one of those plants about which those whose passion it is to name things cannot make up their minds. Its Latin name has changed several times over the years, but whatever it is called when you find it, it is worth looking out for. The yellow archangel is a close relative of the white dead nettle (*Lamium album*). It has whorls of large, nettle-like, bright-yellow flowers in the axils of the upper leaves from April to July, the unbranched flowering stems rising from creeping stems that spread quite widely, if allowed. It looks good in spring with bluebells (*Hyacinthoides non-script*) and stitchwort (*Stellaria holostea*) in a shady spot.

Height: Up to 60cm (24in), but commonly around 25cm (10in).

Habitat: Deciduous woodland and shady banks, especially on lime-rich soils.

Garden care: Water in well when planting. Dead-head regularly to extend the flowering season and to prevent self-seeding. Dig up and divided every couple of years.

Propagation: Seed and plants are available from nurseries and some garden centres. Seed can be saved from existing plants. Plants can be dug up and divided every two to three years. As for other perennials, seed should be sown in spring or summer where it is to flower, or in pots or trays outside to be planted out in the autumn or early in the following spring. The seed needs a period of cold before it will germinate.

SHADE PLANTS

	HEIGHT	FLOWERING SEASON	FLOWER COLOUR
Anemone – Wood	20cm (8in)	March–May	White
Bluebell	45cm (18in)	April–May	Blue
Daffodil	35cm (14in)	Feb–April	Yellow
Enchanter's Nightshade	60cm (24in)	July–Sept	White
Fern – Hart's Tongue	30cm (12in)	n/a	n/a
Fern – Male	1.5m (5ft)	n/a	n/a
Forget-me-not – Wood	35cm (14in)	April–July	Blue
Foxglove	1.5m (5ft)	May–Aug	Pink
Herb Robert	50cm (20in)	May–Dec	Pink
Lily-of-the-valley	30cm (12in)	April–May	White
Lords and Ladies	50cm (20in)	April–May	Purple
Lungwort	30cm (12in)	April–June	Blue/red
Pendulous Sedge	1.5m (5ft)	May–June	Orange/red
Pimpernel – Yellow	7.5cm (3in)	May–Sept	Yellow
Poppy – Welsh	35cm (14in)	May–Sept	Yellow
Primrose	20cm (8in)	Feb–May	Yellow
Ramsons	40cm (16in)	April–June	White
Snowdrop	15cm (6in)	Jan–March	White
Solomon's Seal	60cm (24in)	May–June	White
Sorrel – Wood	12cm (5in)	April–May	Pink/white
Stinking Hellebore	75cm (30in)	Feb–May	Green
Stitchwort – Greater	60cm (24in)	April–June	White
Violet – Common Dog	20cm (8in)	March–May	Violet
Woodruff	30cm (12in)	April–May	White
Wood Sedge	60cm (24in)	May–July	Yellow
Yellow Archangel	60cm (24in)	April–July	Yellow

Chapter Eight

Trees and Climbers

Trees and Climbers

Althoough almost every garden has its share of climbers, including native ones, many people are cautious of using trees in their gardens nowadays. Architects use them in giving overall plans to modern estates and in giving new office complexes, which are often built in ultra-modern style, a natural element, but we seem to have something of an aversion to placing something of such scale in our gardens. This is difficult to understand because trees do so much more than offer shade. They give a sense of scale to the buildings as well as to the garden itself. They provide intimacy in ways that shrubs, hedges, fences and climbers cannot. Trees help to enclose a garden, define its space and give shelter from that great expanse of blue above, making a garden feel more like an outside room, rather than a broad, open expanse. And beyond all that, they can provide interest in the garden through most – and in some cases all – of the seasons with attractive bark, blossom, leaves and berries.

Dog rose

Jack-by-the-hedge

Honeysuckle

<u>Summer-</u>
<u>flowering</u>
<u>Climbers</u>

Among Britain's native trees, of which there are over thirty, there are many very decorative species and varieties. Some are small, barely more than bushes, and others huge, up to well over 33m (100ft) tall, such as the scots pine (*Pinus sylvestris*) or the common oak (*Quercus robur*). These, of course, are not for the average suburban garden, though they are certainly handsome plants and are worthy of use where there is space.

We have over a dozen native climbers, too, and innumerable cultivated varieties of some of them, such as ivy (*Hedera helix*) and honeysuckle (*Lonicera periclymenum*). These can clothe walls, fences, pergolas and arches as well as free-standing obelisks or shrubs with a short season of interest. Some are evergreen, others not. Indeed, though they reach a height of several metres some are herbaceous, dying back to ground level each winter. The everlasting sweet pea (*Lathyrus sylvestris*) and the hop (*Humulus lupulus*) are common examples of this latter group.

BLOSSOMING IN MAY

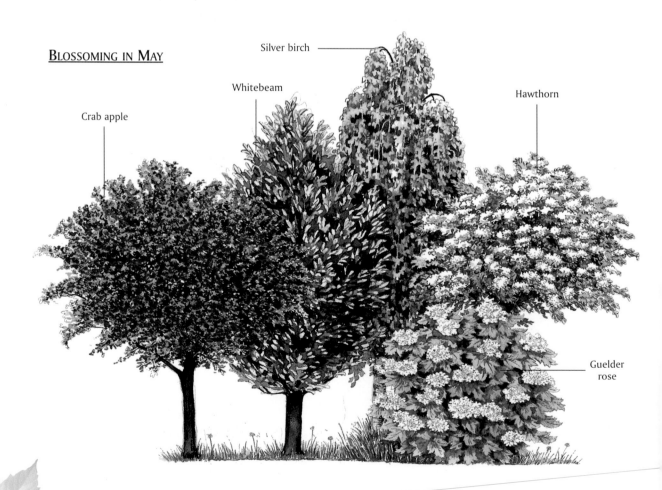

Crab apple

Whitebeam

Silver birch

Hawthorn

Guelder rose

It is the trees and climbers which bring the greenery up off the ground and attract birds into our gardens, giving them places to perch, to roost and to nest as well as often to feed. There are a whole host of things which go to making up a garden and making it feel like part of a home, but one of the essentials has to be birdsong, as attested by the thousands of bird tables, nest boxes and bird baths sold every year. And where would the birds be without somewhere to stand and preen, somewhere to raise their young and somewhere to feed or to sit and watch for food from? The answer, of course, is simple: elsewhere. So, take courage in your hands and choose carefully for a tree, like a dog, is for life and not just for Christmas. Then go out and visit your local nurseries and garden centres, looking for healthy, well-proportioned specimens, and take the plunge. But when you buy a tree, do not buy just one, for it will look odd and lonely; instead, buy two or three, either of the same type or contrasting ones. Then plant them well and enjoy the fruits of your labour.

In making your choice, you can visit some of the most beautiful places in Britain for inspiration. Parks, arboretums, forests and woods will all provide that much-needed preview of what you can expect when your own trees mature.

AUTUMN

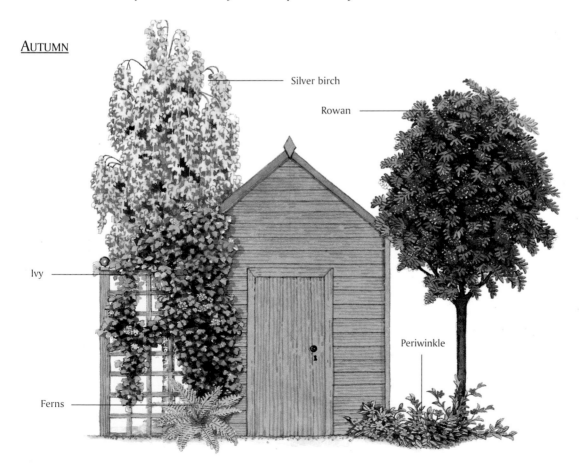

Silver birch

Rowan

Ivy

Periwinkle

Ferns

Alder

Alnus glutinosa

Often seen growing with willows, the alder is a moisture-loving tree, with similar nodules on its roots to those of the pea family. As with the peas, these contain nitrogen-fixing bacteria. The long, yellow male catkins appear at the same time as the rounded, dark-brown, cone-like female ones. They are formed in the previous summer, before the leaves fall, but do not develop fully until February or March and are prominently displayed before the new leaves emerge.

The leaves are held alternately on long stalks from the pale-grey twigs and are quite round, with finely toothed edges and a well-defined indentation in the tip. Decorative cut-leaved varieties have been bred for garden and park use: these have leaves which are deeply divided into six or seven sharply pointed segments. The bark of the alder is rough and furrowed, and dark brown in colour. The trunk is straight, but covered in shrubby foliage, especially on mature trees. Alder can be pollarded and the young shoots will have a purplish colour which contrasts well with the yellow twigs of some of the willows or certain varieties of dogwood (*Cornus sanguinea*).

Height: A fair-sized tree, the alder can attain 12m (40ft) or more.

Habitat: Prefers damp soil and plenty of light, but can be found in drier situations and in shady oak woods.

Garden care: Plant in damp or wet ground and if a full sized tree is not what you require, then pollard it or coppice it every three years after the first five. Surprisingly disease resistant, any problems can generally be cut out with a good pair of loppers or a pruning saw, especially if caught early.

Propagation: Plants are available from nurseries, both in natural and cut-leaved forms. Semi-ripe cuttings can be taken in summer, cutting to just below a leaf node and planting in a sheltered spot in the ground. Seed can be saved and sown in damp compost outdoors when fresh, though it will be some time before a usable plant results from this.

Ash – Common   *Fraxinus excelsior*

The common ash is easily identified in any season. Its bark is pale grey and only lightly fissured. The buds of both leaves and flowers are black, pointed ovals and can be found on the twigs at any time of year. The flowers, which appear before the leaves in April or May, are pinkish bunches of tiny ovaries or stamens without petals, held near the tips of the twigs. The seeds are in the form of 'keys' – that is, each seed is individually held on a stalk and has a slender, twisted papery wing attached to it. These are released in the winter, but can often be seen on the tree well into the following summer, forming dead-looking little bunches among the leaves. The leaves themselves are divided like those of the rowan (*Sorbus aucuparia*). There are usually nine leaflets, each slender, pointed and sharply toothed at the edges, the whole leaf being up to 30cm (12in) long. The leaves of the ash are the last to appear in late spring, often into late May, and they fall in October, having turned pale yellow a few weeks before. There is a weeping variety called 'Pendula', which is very popular in gardens and parks, as well as the natural type and a range of varieties with decoratively coloured leaves.

Height: Usually up to 18m (60ft), though it can approach twice that in ideal conditions.

Habitat: Often found at the edges of flowing water or fresh lakes, it will also grow well in woodland, in hedgerows or on dry slopes.

Garden care: A tough tree, the ash suffers very little from pests and diseases, though it does have one down-side: it suckers freely, especially if coppiced or pollarded. In common with other plants that sucker, these need to be pulled off from the point of origin on the root. Water in well when planting and stake low down to allow a good root system to develop.

Propagation: Saplings are available from nurseries. Hardwood cuttings can be taken in late summer and rooted in a sheltered spot in the garden. The seeds germinate freely in the garden or in pots of compost.

Beech – Common   *Fagus sylvatica*

The buds and leaves of the Beech are similar in appearance to those of the hornbeam (*Carpinus betulus*). However, while the leaves of the latter tree are toothed, those of the beech are just lightly rippled along the edges and while the buds of the hornbeam are held tight along the twigs, those of the beech stand away on short stalks. The bark of the beech is smooth and usually grey. The branches begin low down on the trunk (very conveniently for small boys who wish to climb the tree) and the roots are prominent on the surface of the soil that surrounds the tree. This magnificent tree is not one for small gardens unless it is being used as a hedge, to which it adapts very successfully. The trunk of a mature tree can have a girth of over 6m (20ft), but maturity is slow in coming. The beech can live for three hundred years. Its leaves are held alternately along the somewhat zigzagging stem and are bright green on both sides, unless the highly decorative copper beech (*F. s.* 'Purpurea') is used, when they are a deep, mahogany bronze colour. In late autumn they turn a rich orange and are held on the branches well into the winter, especially if it is mild.

Height: Up to 33m (100ft) as a mature tree. Also useful as a hedging shrub, when it can be kept to 2m (6ft) high quite comfortably.

Habitat: Prefers deep soil, loam or chalk. Often found on hills, where the soil is dry.

Garden care: Firm in well when planting and give the plant plenty of water. Then stand back and enjoy it, as few pests or diseases will trouble it. If using it for a hedge, it can be clipped twice a year to keep it to size, however clipping should not be done until the hedge is about 15cm (6in) taller than is required.

Propagation: Usually sold in autumn and winter as bare-rooted plants, which look dead when you buy them but are not. Beech is freely available from nurseries and garden centres in a variety of forms. Hardwood cuttings can be taken in late summer and rooted in the garden, but they are best left until the following autumn for transplanting, after the leaves have changed if not fallen.

Birch – Silver

Betula pendula

One of the three most popular of our native trees for garden use, along with the cherry plum (*Prunus cerasifera*) and the rowan (*Sorbus aucuparia*). The silver birch is one of two native birches, the other being the downy birch (*B. pubescens*), which has a darker trunk more like that of the wild cherry (*Prunus avium*), and diamond-shaped leaves instead of the distinctly triangular ones of the silver birch. It is the silver-white bark of the trunk which gives the silver birch its common name, while the Latin specific is descriptive of the pendulous nature of its dark reddish branches and twigs. The trunk tends to grow straight and slender, the tree having an elegant if delicate appearance though it is one of the hardiest trees in the world, growing at higher altitudes than almost any other deciduous tree. The triangular leaves are sharply double serrated along the sides, on long stalks, the upper surface mid-green, while the underneath is paler. Tight, purplish male catkins about 4cm (1.5in) long and tiny green female ones are born in April and May, the winged seeds being released in winter, long after the leaves have turned yellow and fallen.

Height: Up to 33m (100ft) in exceptional circumstances, though more usually about half that or less.

Habitat: The silver birch will grow in deciduous or mixed forests, on heathland or on sandy or gravelly soil. It prefers drier conditions than the downy birch, but can tolerate acid or alkaline soils.

Garden care: This tough and adaptable tree needs very little looking after. It should be watered in well and staked low down when planted, to allow the roots to establish better. High winds will knock off some of the thinner twigs, which will need to be tidied up, as will the autumn leaves, when they have fallen, though the tree is far more tolerant of exposed conditions than its appearance would indicate.

Propagation: The trees are easily available from nurseries and larger garden centres. The seed can be gathered and sown in pots in winter, though the branches are too whippy to make useful cuttings.

Cherry – Bird

Prunus padus

Named because its small, black fruit are edible only by birds, this handsome tree is a a spectacular sight in April or May, when its shiny, dark-brown branches are festooned with long racemes of white blossom while the leaves are still young. The leaves are roughly ovate, with a definite point to the tip and fine serration along the edges. Both the flowers and the leaves give off a smell of bitter almond. The branches of the tree form an attractive conical shape. There are several cultivars with different flowers which have been developed for garden use. These include forms with pink flowers, double flowers and a spectacular one with huge hanging spikes of creamy flowers called 'Waterei'. The fruits of the bird cherry are used as flavouring in cherry brandy and some wines.

Height: Up to 10m (30ft).

Habitat: Woods, scrub and hedgerows at lower altitudes. It is found much farther north than the Wild Cherry (*P. avium*) to which it is related, along with Blackthorn (*P. spinosa*).

Garden care: Can take full sun or shade of larger trees. Water in well; use a stake across the base in exposed positions. Water when needed in the first year. Can be prone to attack by red spider mite, aphids, brown rot, silver leaf and cherry bacterial banker. Due to its size an environmentally friendly cure is not practical, so a spray should be used as soon as problems are seen. Brown rot affects mainly the fruit, but also young shoots. The best way to deal with this to remove and discard all affected material immediately. The same applies with silver leaf. Infected material should be burnt or placed in the dustbin. Pruning in the warmest months of the year will lessen the chances of silver leaf attack.

Propagation: Plants are available from nurseries and some garden centres. Hardwood cuttings can be taken in summer and heeled in in a shady spot to shoot by next spring.

Cherry Plum

Prunus cerasifera

The cherry plum flowers with the blackthorn (*P. spinosa*) in February and March, opening its stalked white blossoms with their prominent reddish anthers before the leaves emerge from their buds. Reputed to be one of the original parents of the modern domestic plum (*P. domestica*), this tree, with its smooth, dark bark, resembles the blackthorn more closely in its general form. Its foliage is thinner and the leaves larger, rounded, with finely toothed edges and a definite point at the tip. It bears cherry-like fruit on short stalks in bunches along the twigs in late summer and autumn, before the leaves turn yellow and fall for the winter. The best-known form of the cherry plum is probably the purple-leaved 'Atropurpurea' or 'Pissardii' variety, which originated as a sport in a Persian garden tended by the Frenchman Pissard during the late nineteenth century. This is grown in gardens as an alternative to the copper beech (*Fagus sylvatica* 'Purpurea'), which becomes a much more substantial tree if allowed, though like the cherry plum it can be cut regularly and maintained as a hedging shrub. As well as the dark reddish foliage, 'Atropurpurea' has pale-pink blossom, instead of white.

Height: Up to 8m (24ft) as a tree, though it can be cut and used as a hedge of 2m (6ft) high.

Habitat: Most often seen in hedgerows, it can also be found in woodland on normal to dry soils.

Garden care: Clipping into a shrub will induce suckering, so those suckers appearing outside of the line of the hedge need pulling off. The cherry plum can be attacked by those diseases which affect cherries and plums such as cherry bacterial canker and silver leaf. In the former, leaves develop small round holes, then turn yellow. The trunk and branches develop cankers and whole branches can abruptly die. Affected branches must be cut off immediately and the wound treated with a bituminous wound dressing. Silver leaf is a fungal disease whose name is sufficient description. It is best avoided by pruning only at the height of summer, but if contracted affected branches must be cut back well beyond any sign of infection and the wound dressed with a sealing compound. Brown rot affects mainly the fruit, but can also get into the leaves and wood, and again requires pruning out. Having said all this, these diseases are not common, especially if the tree is well looked after and healthy.

Propagation: Plants are available from nurseries and garden centres. The fruit can be gathered and sown in pots of compost in autumn, left outside to germinate over winter. Hardwood cuttings can be taken in autumn and rooted in a shady spot in the garden.

Cherry – Wild

Prunus avium

Also called the gean, the wild cherry is the parent of edible cherry trees and is still used as the grafting rootstock for them. A wonderful sight in woods through April and May, the wild cherry provides a spectacular show of white blossom. Though each tree flowers for only two or three weeks, the display is worth growing the tree for on its own, even without the shiny chestnut-brown bark with its thin horizontal cracks, the small fruits in mid summer and the fiery blaze of crimson as the leaves turn in autumn. The tree is generally conical in shape. Its leaves are elliptical and sharply pointed at the tips, the margins toothed. Like the blossom, they are borne in bunches along the stems. The leaf stalks are short while the flower stalks are up to 4cm (1.5in) long. The wild cherry is a fast grower, though not large. This last fact is fortunate for those who like the fruits, for the tree will need to be netted if you are to beat the birds to them.

Height: Up to 13m (45ft), though often less. It can be pruned to shape and size, if required.

Habitat: Naturally found in woods and occasionally hedgerows, usually on chalk or limestone soils. Tolerates shade well, though it is equally happy in the sun.

Garden care: Water in well when planting and use a low stake. The cherries can be prone to a number of diseases, though these generally affect trees already under stress rather than those grown in ideal conditions to begin with. See the Garden care section of cherry plum for further details, as these trees suffer from the same ailments.

Propagation: Saplings are available from nurseries and some garden centres, though in the latter, you will be much more likely to find the oriental flowering cherries. Semi-ripe cuttings can be taken in summer and rooted in a sheltered spot in the garden or fruit can be potted up in compost kept damp by sealing in a plastic bag until germination.

Crab Apple

Malus sylvestris

Related to the roses, this small tree has spines along its grey-brown twigs. These have obviously been bred out in the process of producing the cultivated apples, of which this is the main, or perhaps the sole, parent. The leaves are also reminiscent of the rose family, being ovate with serrated edges. They are a mid-green in colour, opening in April from reddish, hairy buds and turning a bright yellow in autumn. The blossom follows the leaves in late April and is borne in small bunches above the leaves, the five petals usually white with a pinkish tinge to the backs. The fruit, 4cm (1.5in) across, is a miniature yellowish apple, sometimes with a hint of red to the skin. They are hard and bitter, but used for crab apple jelly as well as jam and wine. The head of the tree is roughly round in shape, with the growing shoots coming vertically from the top, long and slender, while the fruiting shoots are short.

There are several garden cultivars of the crab apple, grown for their ornamental value. Most are at least partly derived from Asian or North American parentage. They include some varieties with purple leaves, red or pink flowers, ones with red buds that open to white flowers and several different fruit colours.

Height: Up to 10m (30ft), but often smaller. Can be kept in check by pruning out the long growing shoots which come out of the top of the crown.

Habitat: Naturally found in hedgerows and woods. Dry to normal soil conditions, sun or shade.

Garden care: Planting requirements are the same as most trees: water in well and stake if exposed to the wind. Apples, whether wild or cultivated, are prone to a number of diseases and different pests. These are best dealt with as soon as they are noticed, so that they do not weaken the tree. There are several relatively eco-friendly insecticides on the market now to deal with pests. Fungal, viral and bacterial diseases are best dealt with by removing infected tissue and destroying it. Under no circumstances should such material be composted. However, if the tree is in good condition, this will make it less prone to most problems in the first place. Give the tree space for the air to flow around it. Feed it once a year if the soil is not particularly fertile. Water it if there is a prolonged dry spell, especially if it is being grown in close association with other plants, including grass. Prune out old or crossing branches from the centre of the tree, remembering to cut right back to the joint and make the cut as flush as possible with the surrounding wood. Pruning is best done in summer, when the tree is actively growing and so will heal more quickly.

Propagation: Plants are available from nurseries and garden centres. If you already have one, or have access to one, you can plant the seed yourself, as many children still do, but it will be a long time before you have a significant garden tree, even if you plan to train it into a fan or espalier.

Field Maple

Acer campestre

Our native member of the acer family is much smaller than the other two species that grow wild in Britain, having been introduced two to four hundred years ago. These are the sycamore (*A. pseudoplatanus*) and the Norway maple (*A. platanoides*), both of whose Latin names allude to the similarity of these trees to another introduced species, the plane tree (*Platanus orientalis*). All have distinctly acer-like divided palmate leaves, but those of the field maple have rounded, rather than pointed, tips to the lobes. The leaf has three main lobes and two minor ones at the base. Each main lobe is indented one to four times. The field maple makes a good hedgerow plant as well as a very attractive tree, if allowed to mature. In spring the yellow flowers are borne in loose clusters as the orangy-pink leaves emerge, so that the whole tree blazes orange in the sunshine. The mature leaves are a fresh, bright green, turning to amber in autumn. The branches are sinuously curved, the bark finely fissured and light brown.

Height: If allowed to mature into a tree, the field maple can achieve 18m (60ft), though it rarely gets to more than half that. It can be cut regularly to make a bush or hedge, which is best kept to about 2m (6ft).

Habitat: Almost any soil and situation will suit the field maple, though it prefers soil that is not too wet and a sunny aspect.

Garden care: The acers can be prone to a number of diseases. Tar spot is a leaf fungus, producing black marks, usually on the undersides of the leaves. Galls can also affect the leaves, as can rust diseases and black spot. Apart from black spot, these affect the looks rather than the health of the tree, but all can be pruned out and the affected parts destroyed. A well-kept tree should not have such problems anyway.

Propagation: Young trees are available from nurseries. The almost horizontally held seeds will freely germinate, though they are less of a nuisance than those of the sycamore. Hardwood cuttings can be taken in late summer and rooted over winter in a sheltered spot in the garden.

Hornbeam

Carpinus betulus

One of the more useful of our native trees, the hornbeam is also very decorative. Its name derives from the Old English words for 'hard' and 'tree' and the wood is still used for butcher's blocks, skittles and mallets. The tree can become quite large if conditions allow, but is also commonly used for hedging, when it will form a dense, neat growth which has the advantage over beech (*Fagus sylvatica*) that it will retain some of its dead leaves through the winter. Its leaves look a little like those of beech, but are toothed, like those of the elms. The buds in spring look very like those of the beech, but can be distinguished by the fact that they lie tight to the twigs and often begin to open before those of the beech.

The tree bears both male and female flowers on the same twigs, the female ones being at the tips while the male catkins are held a few centimetres further back. The flowers open in April or May and give rise, later in the season, to bunches of winged nut-like fruits. The bark of the trunk is pale greyish-brown and smooth, the trunk itself deeply fluted in a spiral pattern. The smaller twigs are a deep, rich brown in colour and show up well against the pale green of the young leaves, which deepen their colour as the summer progresses. The cultivated variety 'Fastigiata' is widely used in parks and avenues and has a handsome tulip-like shape, its branches curving elegantly upwards.

Height: Up to 26m (78ft), but often coppiced, pollarded or used for hedging.

Habitat: Naturally found in beech and oak woods, where it can tolerate deep shade. Grows well on most soil types, including chalk, but is best on clay, in sun or shade.

Garden care: Water in well when planting. If growing as a hedge, clip once a year in July.

Propagation: Available from garden centres and nurseries. In late autumn and winter, sold as bare-rooted saplings, which look dead as they hold their leaves but usually take well, shooting in March or April. Seed can be saved from existing trees and sown outdoors in autumn, the seedlings transplanted in the following spring.

Lime – Common   *Tilia x europaea*

Potentially the tallest of Britain's broad-leaved trees, the common lime is a hybrid between two native species of lime, the large-leaved lime (*T. platyphyllus*) and the small-leaved lime (*T. cordata*), neither of which is now common. The common lime is a lovely tree, often used in parks and town streets, roughly pyramidal in overall shape, the dark-grey trunk straight and upright. The leaves are broad and almost heart-shaped, though without any indentation at the base, up to 10cm (4in) long and bright green. The tree flowers in early July, when the bright-yellow, sweetly scented flowers are held in small bunches at the tips of the twigs; these flowers are very attractive to bees.

Height: Potentially up to 43m (130ft) in deep, loamy soil, though it averages around 23m (69ft).

Habitat: Limes like deep soil with plenty of nutrients, such as is often found in river valleys in lowland areas. They need good air flow around the leaves, so are not trees of the forest but of open ground.

Garden care: Limes are tall and densely leaved, providing plenty of shade. However, the common lime is not at its best in towns, for the air pollution renders it prone to attack by aphids, which cause it to drip sap on to the ground beneath. A black mould then grows on this, while the tops of the leaves can develop orangy nail galls in response to the puncturing of the sap-sucking insects. However, these problems are far less likely in a rural setting.

Propagation: Young trees are available from nurseries. Semi-ripe cuttings can be taken in summer and rooted in a sheltered spot in the garden, to be transplanted the following spring. Being a cross between the two now-rare natural limes, the common lime is not usually fertile. There are no seed to be collected, but those of either parents are held in small, brown, nut-like fruits. If the seed is sown, the seedling will be seen to have strange hand-shaped seed leaves.

RAMSGATE

Oak – English

Quercus robur

The gnarled and twisted dark reddish-brown branches of the English oak clothed in leaves is an essentially British sight. The English oak is one of many species worldwide and one of two native to the British Isles. The other is the much straighter and more upright sessile oak (*Q. petraea*), which is generally found in the less fertile and wetter regions of the north and north-west, such as Scotland, the Lake District and the Pennines, though also in the New Forest and on Exmoor further south. The term 'sessile' refers to the fact that the acorns of this tree are unstalked, unlike its close relative. The bark of this tree is also much paler, though similar in texture, being finely cracked and vertically ridged. Both trees are large, eventually achieving 33m (100ft) or more, so are suited only to large gardens and parklands, but given that amount of space it would be almost criminal to ignore the majestic rounded form of this tree with its distinctive lobed leaves. The oak flowers in a similar fashion to the hazels, with long, drooping catkins of male flowers and tiny, erect female flowers above them near the tips of the branches. The catkins are borne in bunches, the flowers grouped loosely along their length. This is a tree for those with a long-term view of life, but when you consider its maximum life-span of over a thousand years, it begins to breed relatively young, setting its first acorns at around sixty years. However, it forms an attractive tree from an early age. Its leaves take on a lovely yellow hue through the autumn and are held well into winter.

Height: Up to 40m (120ft), though it grows only slowly and will take around a hundred years to achieve this stature, even on the deep soils which allow it. On more rocky or windswept ground, it will barely achieve a fifth of that height and its twisted and distorted trunk will grow to suit the conditions.

Habitat: At home on most soils, it is less common on chalk and limestone. The oak will thrive on a deep clay soil, but will also take root in the craggy, boulder-strewn river valleys of Exmoor and Wales, where its twisted branches provide shelter and home for mosses, ferns and other plants. It will colonize cleared areas of woodland, competing well with other trees and shrubs as well as even the most vigorous of grasses. The sturdy seedlings can also be found on the edges of pastureland and in hedgerows.

Garden care: Little care is needed by this tough tree. Allowance must be made for its potential size when choosing a site. The main disease of the oak is the oak-apple or gall, which is a growth formed in response to a parasitic wasp. This gall-fly lays its eggs under the soft bark of the twigs, causing a round swelling of the sap-wood which contains the larva of the insect. Prune out affected shoots as soon as they are found and burn or remove from the site.

Propagation: Saplings are available from nurseries, usually as pot-grown plants. If you already have a specimen, then semi-ripe cuttings can be taken with a heel and potted up after dipping into hormone rooting powder, or the acorns can be planted in pots and the seedlings cared for in this way until they are large enough to plant out.

Rowan

Sorbus aucuparia

Also known as the mountain ash, for the superficial resemblance of its leaves to those of the ash (*Fraxinus excelsior*), it is debated whether the name rowan is derived from the Norse word for 'charm' and related to its long association with witchcraft or from the Gaelic for 'red one', referring to its copious autumn berries. The ash can be separated from the rowan by the fact that the leaflets of the rowan are finer and their edges serrated, while those of the ash are smooth. A tough, hardy tree, the rowan is often seen in mountainous regions, sometimes clinging to the most precarious positions on scree slopes or almost vertical rock faces, where a seed may have been dropped into a crevice by a bird. The bark of the slender trunk is smooth and grey.

The pale-green, feathery foliage appears in April and is followed in May or June by the broad, flattened heads of small white flowers, spread evenly over the tree. The flowers have a pleasant smell and it is these which give away the tree's close relationship to the whitebeam (*S. aria*) and the wild service tree (*S. torminalis*), though the leaves of all three are very different. The berries begin to form as soon as the flowers are shed and by August have fully ripened into the familiar clusters of red pea-sized spheres which look very decorative against the orangy-yellow of the autumn leaves. There are several modern varieties, bred with different-coloured leaves and/or berries, such as 'Autumn Glow', which has pinkish-yellow fruits and fiery red autumn foliage.

Height: Up to 10m (30ft).

Habitat: A very adaptable tree, the rowan will grow just about anywhere, from exposed mountainsides to the rich loam of southern river valleys, also in open woodland. Being fairly open in habit, it will allow grass and other plants to grow very close to the trunk without shading them out too much.

Garden care: Like all trees, the rowan will benefit from a stake angled across the base of its trunk when first planted as a sapling and like all plants, it will benefit from watering in well at this time, but having done this, as long as it does not get too hot for too long in the early months, the rowan will look after itself and, once established, will grow away happily.

Propagation: Bare-rooted or pot-grown saplings of the native tree or the several cultivars are easily available from garden centres and nurseries. Bare-rooted trees are best planted in autumn or in a mild spell in winter. Pot-grown ones can be planted at any time, as long as they are watered in well. Cuttings can be taken in summer or autumn, or the berries can be harvested and sown in a pot in a sheltered spot to overwinter and germinate in spring.

Whitebeam

Sorbus aria

Named by the Saxons, this small to medium-sized tree is highly decorative for much of the year as well as being able to withstand dry conditions, pollution and the salt winds of a coastal garden. The 'beam' part of the name is simply Saxon for tree; the leaves that give it the other part of its name are fairly large and elliptical, with fine teeth along the edges and the characteristic downy whiteness underneath.

The top sides of the whitebeam's leaves are pale in spring, darkening with maturity, then in autumn turning a rich russet colour along with the scarlet red of the berries. The sweet-scented white flowers, borne in large, tight bunches at the tips of the twigs, appear in April and May. The bark is smooth, with horizontal ridged scales a little like the cherries and a light, pinkish-grey colour.

Height: Up to 13m (45ft), but often smaller, with a neat, compact habit.

Habitat: The whitebeam naturally grows in open woodland with the shelter of close association with other trees, generally on chalk or limestone soils. However, it also thrives on sunny slopes and dry soils, where its hairy leaves help it resist water loss. In recent years it has taken over somewhat from the limes as a street tree, due to its compact shape and good resistance to pollution.

Garden care: Like all trees, the whitebeam will benefit from a low stake when young, in order to allow the roots to establish a good hold. If space is restricted, it can be pruned to size once a year, preferably in early spring just before the sap rises, as the whitebeam flowers on the current year's growth.

Propagation: Young trees are available from nurseries and garden centres. As for most trees and shrubs, pot-grown specimens can be planted at any time of year, as long as they are watered in well and not allowed to dry out in the first few months. Bare-root plants are best planted in winter, as long as the ground is not frozen or snow-covered. Semi-ripe cuttings can be taken in late summer, being pulled from the tree with a heel of older wood, which is then trimmed to around 2.5cm (1in) long, dipped in hormone rooting powder and potted in a fairly free-draining compost in a sheltered spot. Rooting should be well advanced by autumn.

Willow – Pussy

Salix caprea

A tree of many names, the pussy willow is also known as the goat willow, goat palm or sallow. A weeping variety found growing in Scotland in 1840 is known as the Kilmarnock willow and is grown widely in gardens. Uniquely among British willows, the pussy willow has broad, ovate leaves. These are a bluish green in colour and the undersides felted with fine white hairs. The leaves appear after the catkins, which bloom in March and April. There are male and female trees and it is the males that bear the classic short, oval catkins, covered in hairy white flowers with prominent bright-yellow stamens. It is the females, however, which gave the tree its popular name, for though they are less conspicuous than the males their catkins are larger and, once fertilized, covered with a dense coat of silver hair. Prior to this the catkins of the female tree are coarse and pale green. This is an invaluable tree for bee-keepers, for it is one of the first to blossom in the spring and provide a source of nectar for the early bees.

Height: It is debatable whether this should be classed as a large shrub or a small tree. To a large extent this depends on its growing conditions, but with one stem or several, pussy willow rarely exceeds 10m (30ft) in height.

Habitat: Found naturally on woodland edges, in clearings and on slopes, it is most at home on damp soil, especially beside open water or in a ditch or stream.

Garden care: The willows have quick-growing and long roots which establish good anchorage before the branches become too large or numerous, so staking is unlikely to be needed. Pruning can be done just to keep the tree tidy and to remove any crossing branches or to take sprays of catkins for indoor display in spring.

The young shoot tips can be prone to attack by blackfly in summer. A spray of soapy water or if the infestation is bad, a proprietary aphid spray should deal with these effectively. Otherwise little care is needed.

Propagation: Plants are available from nurseries and garden centres. Cuttings 30cm (12in) long can be taken and pushed into the ground after stripping the majority, though not all, of the leaves. Use stems about 1cm (0.4in) thick, and cut below a bud or leave a heel if taking to the base of the stem: nearly all will root. Seed can be sown if you have a female tree. Sow in damp sterile compost in late spring and pot on when large enough to handle. Germination rate is usually very good.

Willow – White

Salix alba

One of the parents of the weeping willow (*S. Babylonica*), this fairly tall tree, along with the white poplar (*Populus alba*) and, to a slightly lesser extent in summer, the whitebeam (*Sorbus aria*), shines silvery white in the summer sun, as if it belongs on the shores of the Mediterranean. Certainly the white willow is happy on the water's edge, but not that of the sea. It is a tree of river and lake banks, and even the shallows of the water, where the trunk puts out a short tracery of bright-red water roots. The white willow is similar in many respects to the crack willow (*S. fragilis*), which is also found in similar habitats, but lacks the silvery undersides to the long, narrow, almost lanceolate leaves. The osier willow (*S. viminalis*) has even longer leaves than these two, but is usually seen as a shrub and has short, yellow catkins like those of the pussy willow (*S. caprea*), instead of the long, downy, white ones of the other species. It is the white willow that provides wood for cricket bats. The bark is thick, deeply fissured and dark, reddish brown, contrasting well with the leaves. The lower branches tend to droop downwards. The tree grows quickly but is readily pollarded, though this loses its natural shape.

Height: Up to 18m (60ft), which can be achieved in fifteen years in good conditions.

Habitat: Wet soil at the edges of rivers and lakes. Also grows in the shallows.

Garden care: Willows can suffer from rust diseases and blackfly attack at the shoot tips, but these only really affect those trees which are under stress already. Blackfly can be washed off with a hosepipe or, if the infestation is too bad, sprayed with an insecticide. A bad case of rust can be pruned out or sprayed with a fungicide.

Propagation: Saplings are available from nurseries. Ripe or semi-ripe cuttings are notoriously easy to root in the ground. Just break off a twig, something between finger thick and 2cm thick, close to a junction. Strip most of the leaves from it and push it into the ground; there is a good chance it will root.

169

Yew – Common   *Taxus baccata*

One of only three native conifers in Britain, the common yew is the one found in southern parts, while the scots pine (*Pinus sylvestris*) and the juniper (*Juniper communis*) are generally found naturally in northern England and Scotland. The common yew is noted for its great longevity and its slow growth, as well as for being poisonous. There is a common yew in Tayside, Scotland, which is thought to be around two thousand years old and a common yew hedge in Gloucestershire which is nearly two hundred and eighty years old and stands 12m (40ft) high. These extremes, however, are not what we are seeking as gardeners. For us, the yew is a useful hedging or topiary plant, the dense coating of dark leaflets, held in opposite pairs on the narrow, pliable stems lending themselves well to close clipping. The habit, unusual among the conifers, of bearing branches from very low on the trunk also helps in this pursuit, allowing the tree to be shaped into almost any form the gardener desires. The thin, reddish bark, the needles once they are clipped, and the seed are all poisonous, though the flesh of the bright-red berries is fortunately not. If allowed to grow as a tree, the common yew will not grow excessively large, though the trunk will become very wide and gnarled.

Height: No more than 16m (48ft), even at an old age, but can be clipped to whatever size is required.

Habitat: Mainly found on chalk or limestone soils, the yew can grow in the open as a parkland tree or as an understorey tree in a forest situation, tolerating quite deep shade.

Garden care: The tree flowers in February, the tree being either male or female, and the berries appear in autumn, so any clipping must take this into account if berries are required to add to the decorative effect of the tree. Disease and drying out are not problems for the yew, but clippings must be raked up and disposed of in the dustbin or bonfire.

Propagation: Saplings are available from nurseries and some garden centres. Pencil-thick to finger-thick cuttings can be taken, trimmed to a joint at the beak and dipped into hormone rooting powder before being planted into drained ground. About 50 per cent should grow.

Honeysuckle

Lonicera periclymenum

Also known as woodbine, this excellent climber flowers between June and September. It has cream flowers tinged with yellow and pink, borne in clusters of six or more. These are highly scented and full of nectar and are followed by clusters of unpalatable bright red berries. The woody stems climb by twisting clockwise around whatever support is available. The plant is deciduous, with small, soft green leaves along the stem.

Height: Up to 6m (20ft).

Habitat: Widespread in hedgerows and woodland. Well known for its tolerance of shade.

Garden care: Provide firm support. Tie in when young and prune as space dictates in spring. Can be prone to black spot and mildew. Proprietary sprays can be used for these. Best planted near to the house, where the gorgeous, rich evening scent can be enjoyed to the full.

Propagation: From seed or cuttings or as plants from a garden centre or nursery. Cuttings can be rooted in well-drained compost with no need for rooting powder, or in a jar of water.

Hop

Humulus lupulus

This herbaceous perennial climber is one of many plants that have been used over the centuries to flavour beer and it is the one which has lasted the test of time. Whether that is a result of its flavour or the ease of its cultivation and harvest is debatable, but in either case it is useful in the garden as well, for decorative purposes. Several thin twining stems arise from the overwintered rootstock in spring, twisting up whatever support is available as they grow rapidly, putting out a profusion of large, jagged-edged leaves with three broad lobes as they go. The male plants have starry yellow flowers in July and August. The female flowers are tiny, green and insignificant, though it is these that will later develop into the yellowy-green, cone-like fruits that are used in brewing. Most often used in the garden is the golden hop (*H. l.* 'Aurea'), which has richly yellowish leaves, especially when grown in full sun.

Height: Up to 5m (15ft), though it dies back to ground level at the end of each year.

Habitat: Probably originally a plant of damp woodland, it can tolerate sun or shade, wet or dry soil, but is usually found on neutral to alkaline ground, such as the chalk of Kent and Sussex.

Garden care: Dig in plenty of organic matter when planting and mulch with well-rotted manure each year afterwards. Chop back any runners that arise from the roots or dig them up and pot them if new plants are required. Cut away dead stems at the end of each year.

Propagation: Plants and seeds are available from garden centres and nurseries. Existing plants can be lifted and divided every three years. If you have a female plant, seed can be saved from it and sown in pots or trays in spring or autumn.

Ivy

Hedera helix

There are countless varieties of ivy for sale in garden centres, nurseries, market stalls and D.I.Y. outlets throughout the country. Some are green-leaved, some yellow-variegated, some silver-variegated; some large, some dwarf. It must be that there is an ivy for practically any situation in which you could possibly wish to put one. It is a popular misconception that ivy can damage walls or trees up which it climbs, but this is not true. It draws no sustenance from trees and, given that the wall is sound in the first place, it will cause no damage to brickwork, for it climbs by means of a glue-like secretion, rather than invasive growths. However, it would be injudicious to grow it up one of the English West Country's cob walls. Ivies are evergreen and, perversely, they flower in the autumn and produce berries in the spring. The flowers are small, greenish-yellow and fairly insignificant, though sweet scented. The berries are held in tight clumps and ripen to a purplish-black colour. Flowers and berries are borne on mature wood, which has crinkled ovoid leaves with pointed tips, rather than the typically ivy-shaped, five-pointed leaves of the younger growth. It can make an excellent wall-cover on its own or act as a contrasting background for other climbers, such as clematis species or hops (*Humulus lupulus*).

Height: The wild species can grow to almost 33m (100ft), the trunks reaching 10cm (4in) thick, but cultivated varieties can be as small as 30cm (12in) long at maturity. It is best to check the label on the type you are buying.

Habitat: Will climb over any support, be it a wall, a tree stump or a living tree. Grows in sun or shade, often on the driest of soils, though it will tolerate a reasonable level of moisture.

Garden care: Water in well when planting, firming the soil around the roots, train in the required direction and, once it is settled, it will grow away strongly. The waxy leaves repel just about any pest or disease attack, so the main care required is to keep the plant in trim, once it has reached its required size.

Propagation: Plants are freely available in just about any outlet. Cuttings can be taken in the warmer months and potted up, the pots sealed in plastic bags until rooting has occurred and the cuttings begin to grow.

Nightshade – Woody

Solanum dulcamara

Also known as bittersweet, this relative of the potato and tomato bears smooth, heart-shaped leaves on long stalks from the thin, dark, twining stems. The main stem is woody at the base, as opposed to that of the black nightshade (*S. nigra*), which has black stems and white flowers, and dies back in winter. The flowers of the woody nightshade are exotic if small, about 1cm (0.3in) long and purple and yellow in colour. They are carried in branched bunches, just two or three of which will be open at any time. This means that the berries

– some of which will be ripe while there are still flowers on the plant – ripen at different times. They are ovoid in shape, about 0.6cm (0.25in) long, start life pale green and ripen to a glowing red, almost semi-transparent. The berries, along with the rest of the plant, are poisonous. So too are the black nightshade (*S. nigrum*) and the deadly nightshade (*Atropa belladona*), which is a medium-sized herbaceous plant, not a climber like the others. Enchanter's nightshade (*Circaea lutetiana*) is not related to these plants and is not poisonous.

Height: Up to 2.1m (7ft).

Habitat: Very adaptable. Grows in sun or shade, in damp or dry soil. Readily found in hedges or on dry slopes, in wet woodland or on shingle beaches.

Garden care: Plant close to some form of support against which the plant can lean or through which it can scramble. Do not plant if small children are going to use the garden, as the very attractive

berries are toxic, if not deadly. However, if this is pointed out most children only need telling once and the plant is distinctive enough that mistakes will not be made.

Propagation: Available from some nurseries. Berries can be picked and potted in compost outside in autumn to germinate in spring, after the cold has broken their dormancy.

Old Man's Beard   *Clematis vitalba*

Also known as wild clematis, or traveller's joy for the frothy abundance of its seed heads through autumn and winter, and virgin's bower for the complex tangle of its interlaced stems, old man's beard is a climbing shrub common in hedgerows in southern Britain, especially on chalk and limestone. It climbs over other shrubs and trees by means of twisting, clinging leaf-stalks, the leaves divided into three lobes, each dark green and heart-shaped. The stems are thin and weak and much branched, but the main trunk can eventually become thick and woody, with a thin, pale bark. White-petalled flowers with a sparkling mass of stamens are about 2.5cm (1in) across and are borne in massed, branched panicles from late June into September. From October onwards its seeds are displayed even more prominently, in little balls of white hair 4cm (1.5in) across, which cloak the plant in silvery light in the low winter sun.

Height: A vigorous and long-lived plant, old man's beard can grow to 10m (30ft), if allowed.

Habitat: Hedgerows and woodland edges, usually on lime or chalk soils, in sun or partial shade.

Garden care: Plant deep, to encourage underground shooting and therefore several stems, as well as for the safety aspect, in case of clematis wilt disease. Treat grey mould or black spot on the leaves promptly, either by removing affected leaves or with a proprietary fungicide. Like other late-flowering clematis varieties, pruning is best done in February, cutting hard back, to within a foot of the ground. Like other small-flowered types, this is a vigorous plant, suitable for large-scale jobs, such as covering a pergola or house-front, or climbing up a large tree.

Propagation: Plants and seed are available from specialist nurseries. Seed can be sown in pots outside in autumn or spring, as for other hardy perennials. Existing plants can be propagated from cuttings taken in June. Clematis species root from internodal cuttings, unlike most other plants; that is to say, the basal cut should be made roughly halfway between leaf nodes, rather than just beneath one.

Sweet Pea – Everlasting

Lathyrus sylvestris

The narrow-leaved everlasting sweet pea is just one of several closely related and fairly similar perennial sweet peas that are native to this country. They are more scrambling than truly climbing like the annual garden varieties, which are all bred from stock introduced from Italy in the late seventeenth century. Their large, showy flowers are pink to purple in colour, sometimes with white markings on the lower petals and held in long-stalked loose bunches of three to six flowers during July and August. They naturally scramble over shrubs or sprawl over the ground, but will happily make their way up and along a picket fence or up the side of an arch through another climber, such as an early-flowering clematis.

Height: Up to 2m (6ft). The Sea Pea (*L. japonicus*), which flowers from June to August, grows to 1m (3ft), while the now-rare Marsh Pea (*L. palustris*), flowering from May to July, reaches up to 1.2m (4ft).

Habitat: Open woodland and scrub. The sea pea scrambles over shingle beaches; the marsh pea inhabits damp scrubland and fens.

Garden care: Provide a suitable support and plenty of sun, dead-head often or pick the flowers for the vase and these plants will reward you with a prolific show of flowers during the season, dying back in autumn, only to reappear from ground level the following spring.

Propagation: Seed and sometimes plants of the everlasting pea are available from the local garden centre. The other species can be obtained from specialist nurseries. Seed needs to be scarified before sowing in late summer or early autumn in pots which can be kept outside.

Vetch – Tufted   *Vicia cracca*

Arguably the most handsome of three closely related species, the tufted vetch is also the tallest, climbing up to around 2m (6ft) through hedges and shrubs and throwing out flower spikes on side branches as it goes. The flowers are bluish purple: there are up to forty flowers on a spike that can be up to 7.5cm (3in) long. The leaves are divided, in the manner of many of the pea family, into a double row of definite ovate leaflets, anything from ten to thirty per leaf. The leaf tips bear branched tendrils, with which the plant climbs. It nearest relatives are the wood vetch (*V. sylvatica*) and the bush vetch (*V. sepium*). The former is almost as tall as tufted vetch, growing up to 1.5m (5ft). Wood vetch is a very adaptable plant, taking to sun or shade, in woods or on mountains or even cliff faces and shingle. Its flowers are fewer but larger, and are pink or white with purplish veining. Unfortunately, it attracts ants. Bush vetch is a smaller plant than the others, growing up to 1m (3ft). It has shorter leaves with far fewer leaflets; its flowers are a rosy purple in colour, larger than those of the tufted vetch but fewer, with only two to six in a spike. It lives on roadsides and in open scrub, as does the tufted vetch. All three are perennial, growing from a rhizome or underground stem.

Height: Up to 2m (6ft).

Habitat: Hedgerows, open scrub and rough grassland.

Garden care: Water in well when planting and dead-head to extend flowering, which can last from early June into September.

Propagation: Seed and plants are available from specialist nurseries. Seed can be saved from existing plants – it is borne in tiny pea-like pods with up to six seeds in each – and needs scarifying, or scratching of the outer coat, before being sown either in autumn or spring in pots or where it is to flower. Plants can be lifted and divided every three years or so.

Vetchling – Meadow   *Lathyrus pratensis*

This weakly climbing perennial has round heads of up to twelve yellow pea-like flowers, about 2.5cm (1in) long, from May to August, followed by narrow, black seed pods. The vetchlings differ from the vetches in having just a few leaflets, arising from a central point, instead of several leaflets borne in a ladder-like arrangement. There are ten species native to these shores, with flowers of pink, red and white, and yellow. The meadow vetchling is by far the most common, forming bright patches of yellow in tall grassland through the summer. It climbs and scrambles by means of twining tendrils in the same manner as the vetches and the sweet peas, to which it is closely related.

Height: Up to 1.2m (4ft) with sufficient support.

Habitat: Dry grassland, scrub and woodland edges.

Garden care: Water in well when planting, placing the plant close to some form of support, be it grasses or other plants. Dead-head to extend flowering season and cut back hard in September. A feed with well-rotted manure or other organic fertilizer in spring will give vigour and strength to the plant.

Propagation: Seed is available from specialist nurseries or can be saved from existing plants and sown in pots in autumn. It needs to be scarified before sowing; that is, the surface of the seed needs to be scratched to aid germination.

TREES AND CLIMBERS

	HEIGHT	FLOWERING SEASON	FLOWER COLOUR
Alder	13m (42ft)	Feb–March	Yellow
Ash – Common	20m (60ft)	April–May	Pink
Beech – Common	30m (100ft)	April	Yellow
Birch – Silver	30m (100ft)	April–May	Purple/green
Cherry – Bird	10m (30ft)	April–May	White
Cherry – Plum	8m (24ft)	Feb–March	White/pink
Cherry – Wild	13m (42ft)	April–May	White
Crab Apple	10m (30ft)	April	Pink
Field Maple	20m (60ft)	April–May	Yellow
Hornbeam	26m (78ft)	April–May	Yellow/green
Lime – Common	43m (130ft)	July	Yellow
Oak – English	30m (100ft)	May	Yellow
Rowan	10m (30ft)	May–June	White
Whitebeam	15m (45ft)	April–May	White
Willow – Pussy	10m (30ft)	March–April	Yellow
Willow – White	20m (60ft)	March–April	Yellow/green
Yew – Common	16m (48ft)	Feb–March	Yellow/green
Honeysuckle	6m (20ft)	June–Sept	Yellow/cream/pink
Hop	5m (15ft)	July–Aug	Yellow/green
Ivy	33m (100ft)	Sept–Oct	Yellow/green
Nightshade – Woody	2.3m (7ft)	June–Sept	Purple/yellow
Old Man's Beard	10m (30ft)	June–Sept	White
Sweet Pea – Everlasting	2m (6ft)	June–Aug	Pink
Vetch – Tufted	2m (6ft)	June–Aug	Blue
Vetchling – Meadow	1.2m (4ft)	May–Aug	Yellow

FURTHER READING

There have been many books published over the years on British wild flowers and on gardening with them. Probably the best known is the *Flora Britannica*, which is a massive volume, regularly updated, but conveniently split into sections which are also published as separate volumes. Also of interest are the following:

The AA Book of the British Countryside (Hodder and Stoughton)
Encyclopedia of Garden Plants and Flowers (Reader's Digest)
Every Day Gardening In Colour Percy Thrower (Hamlyn)
Field Guide to the Trees and Shrubs of Britain (Reader's Digest)
Field Guide to the Wild FLowers of Britain & Northern Europe (Reader's Digest)
Gardens of England and Wales Open for Charity (The National Gardens Scheme)
Geoff Hamilton's Cottage Garden Geoff Hamilton (Ted Smart)
Grasses, Sedges and Rushes in Colour M. Skytte Christiansen (Blandford Press)
Grasses Jo Chatterton (Lorenz Books)
Havens of the Wild (Reader's Digest)
How to Make a Wildlife Garden Chris Baines (Elm Tree Books)
Nature Watcher's Directory David Marsden (Hamlyn)
Observers Book of Wild Flowers Francis Rose (Bloomsbury Books)
RHS Plant Finder (Dorling Kindersley)
RHS Water Gardening Peter Robinson (Dorling Kindersley)
Trees and Shrubs of the British Isles N. Barrie Hodgson (John Crowther)
The Flower Expert Dr D.G. Hessayon (P.B.I.)
The Ultimate Garden Designer Tim Newbury (Ward, Lock)
Wild About the Garden Jackie Benett (Channel 4 Books)
Wild Flower Gardening Michael Jefferson-Brown (Cassell)
Wild Flowers of Britain Roger Phillips (Pan)
Wild Flowers of Britain and Europe W. Lippert and D. Podlech (Collins)

PLACES TO VISIT

TO BUY PLANTS OR SEED

There are many local garden centres and nurseries, usually listed in the Yellow Pages, which stock an assortment of plants and seed for sale, including an increasing range of wild species. However, ones of particular interest here include the following:

Alternatives, Yorkley Wood, Nr. Lydney, Glos.
Arne Herbs, Chew Magna, Avon.
Deanswood Plants, Littlethorpe, Nr. Ripon, N. Yorks.
Dufford Nurseries, Cullompton, Devon.
Honeysome Aquatic Nursery, Sutton, Nr. Ely, Cambs.
Hilton Manor Gardens, Nr. Nolton, Pembs.
Iden Croft Herbs, Staplehurst, Kent.
John Shipton Bulbs, Whitland, Dyfed.
Kingsfield Conservation Nursery, Winsham, Chard, Somerset.
Linda Gascoigne Wild Flowers, Kilsworth Beauchamp, Leics.
Malcoff Cottage Garden Nursery, Malcoff, Chapel-en-le-Frith, Derbys.
Marle Place Plants, Brenchley, Nr. Tonbridge, Kent.
Natural Selection, Hullavington, Chippenham, Wilts.
Patricia Cooper, Mundford, Norfolk.
Perrie Hale Forest Nursery, Honiton, Devon.
Really Wild Flowers, Sutton Waldron, Blandford Forum, Dorset.
The Wildflower Centre, Sisland, Nr. Norwich.
Under The Greenwood Tree, Vernolds Common, Craven Arms, Shrops.

Also, those places already mentioned in the Acknowledgements of this book and, for mail order only, John Chambers Wildflower Seeds, Barton Seagrave, Kettering, Northants.

FOR INSPIRATION

Many of the above have display gardens laid out. The local press and the Yellow Pages have notification of local garden openings throughout the season. Properties of the National Trust and English Heritage are often worth visiting. The National Trust also owns large areas of nature reserves and beauty spots without any architectural or historic properties on them. Local nature reserves can be found through the local library. The Woodland Trust owns and manages some glorious areas throughout the country, which the public are welcome to visit and explore. And we all know of the National Parks, such as the Lake District, the Peak District, Exmoor and Snowdonia. Then there are places like Wisley and Virginia Water in Surrey, the Beth Chatto Gardens, Elmstead Market, Chelmsford, Essex; the late Geoff Hamilton's gardens at Barnsdale, Exton, Nr. Oakham, Rutland; Harlow Carr in Harrogate, Yorks and the Water Gardens at Wembworthy, Chumleigh, Devon. Also Stapely Water Gardens and Bridgemere Garden World, both near Nantwich, Cheshire; Eastgrove Cottage Garden Nursery, Sankyns Green, Nr. Shrawley, Worcs. and Bro-Meigan Gardens, Boncath, Pembs. At most of these you can buy plants as well as viewing the gardens. All are worth visiting if you have the opportunity and in these days of motorways and increased leisure time, at least some will be well within day-trip distance, wherever you live.

Other useful contacts are:
English Nature, Northminster House, Peterborough, Cambs. Tel. 01733 455000
The Wildlife Trusts U.K. National Office, The Green, Witham Park, Waterside South, Lincoln. Tel. 01522 544400

GLOSSARY

Acid Having a pH value below 7, pH being a measure of the concentration of hydrogen ions in a sample.

Alkali Having a pH value above 7, as do hydroxides and caustic soda, for example.

Anther The upper, pollen-holding part of the stamen.

Axil The point at which a leaf or its stalk branches away from the stem.

Bract A modified leaf-like structure which is situated immediately behind the true flower and looks like a petal.

Catkin A narrow, cylindrical collection of tiny flowers, usually all of the same sex.

Coppice To cut a tree down to its stump so that it will grow several new shoots from around that stump, giving a number of young, slender stems instead of the one thick trunk. Can be repeated every seven to twenty years.

Corolla A tube-like arrangement of inner petals.

Cultivar An artificially selected and bred plant which will breed true from seed.

Double-serrated Refers to leaves that have toothed, or serrated, edges, those teeth then having secondary teeth along their edges.

Ericaceous Acidic or acid-loving, as are the Ericaceae family of heathers.

Hard-wood cuttings Segment of mature stem, cut from the plant with the purpose of using it to grow new plants. Usually trimmed at the base to just under a leaf node, then inserted into soil or compost.

Hybrid Offspring of two distinct species or varieties. Often sterile, so cannot reproduce sexually.

Inflorescence A definable group of flowers on a plant.

Internode The length of a stem between two nodes.

Layering Pegging down the stem of a plant into soil or compost, often after wounding the underside of the stem, so that roots will form where stem touches ground and a new plant will be formed.

Leaflet A segment of a divided leaf which has its own defined leaf-like shape.

Lime Referring to soil: that which has a pH in the alkaline range and has a high concentration of calcium salts. Similar in many respects to chalky soil.

Node A joint in the stem of a plant, from where leaves or shoots are formed.

Ovary The female reproductive part of a flower, topped by the stigma.

Palmate Hand-like form of leaf shape.

Panicle A branched group of flowers on a stem.

Perennial Living for more than two years.

Pollard Cutting off the main branches of a tree so that the top of the trunk will produce many small shoots instead of a few large ones.

Raceme A grouping of flowers along a single stem.

Rhizome Thickened horizontal stem which sits at or just under the soil surface and from which the main bulk of the plant will grow up at the beginning of each growing season.

Scarify To scratch or abrade the surface of a seed before sowing, in order to aid germination.

Semi-ripe cutting A length of stem that is cut off in order to make a new plant from it, this stem being not fully mature and woody, but not as green and flexible as the young shoots of the plant.

Serrated With regular, toothlike notches on an edge.

Sharp-drained Soil which contains a lot of sand or grit and so does not hold water.

Soft-wood cutting A cutting taken from the soft, new growth near the tips of the stems of a plant. Generally used for succulent plants.

Stamen The male reproductive parts of a flower.

Stigma The tip of the female reproductive parts of the flower, which receives the pollen.

Stratify To give seed a significant period of cold, such as would be experienced in winter, in order to encourage germination.

Style The tubular section of the female reproductive parts of the flower which connects the stigma to the ovary.

Tendril A modified leaf or stem segment which coils around anything it comes into contact with in order to cling on and lend the plant support.

Umbel A more-or-less flat-topped inflorescence in which the stalks of the flowers radiate from a central point like the ribs of an umbrella.

Whorl Circular arrangement of leaves, petals or other parts of a plant which all radiate from a single point.

ABOUT THE AUTHOR

While Julian Slatcher has always had a love of natural history and farming and has been writing since an early age, his interest in photography did not emerge until the mid 1980s, out of a desire to capture and share the beauty of nature and a lack of ability as an artist. He came to gardening comparatively late, in 1989, when he acquired his first garden and decided it should look as pretty as possible for as much of the year as he could manage. A six-foot square greenhouse produced over 1,000 plants in its first year, and friends and family began to encourage this new-found fascination. Having learned through word of mouth, hands-on experience and the usual books and magazines, this book was born out of a growing realization that many of the plants he was using in the garden were of native British origin. With so many introduced species being used, just how many of our own were left in common garden use? Research produced a startling answer and the seed of an idea was born: to reintroduce people to those native plants that we still use, as well as those that have fallen out of common use. That way, at least some native British plants that are increasingly under threat in the wild may be perpetuated.

Qualified in agriculture and biochemistry, Julian has had a varied career in agriculture, forestry, pathology and engineering. His photos have been published in *Four Shires* magazine, *Garden Answers* and on the B.B.C.'s *Country File* programme, and he also does commercial and advertising photography. His writing is mainly in the fiction arena, but he has also covered scientific subjects, photography and the R.N.L.I. Julian now lives in a village in north Oxfordshire and runs a flourishing photographic business nearby with his partner. He also travels regularly and widely – always with a camera. He is already working on his next book.

Acknowledgements

No book like this can be completed by one person alone and here I would like to acknowledge the help received in the production of this volume from a number of people. I must thank my mother for her help with the artwork roughs and with identification of some of the plants which I found on my travels. Liz Pepperell, the artist, who turned our rough sketches into such magnificent finished drawings. My father for some of the photographs and information on where to find some of the plants. Pru Dunning for some of the additional photography. Toby Pearson of the Woodland Trust in Suffolk and Craig Churchill for information on where to find some of the plants, and Jenny Pearson for helping Pru and me to find some of them when we got there. Also, the staff of the Naturescape Wildflower Farm in Langar, Notts, of Barncrock Nurseries in Longdon, Staffs, and of The Water Garden in Hinton Parva, near Swindon, Wilts., for information and much help in finding plants to photograph. Andy Charman, former Commissioning Editor at the Guild of Master Craftsman Publications Ltd for his genuine interest in the book and the subject which have allowed me to take the initial idea through to final fruition. And all my friends and family for their support and patience while I did so.

Thank you all.

INDEX

Pages with illustrations are given in **bold**.

OTHER TITLES AVAILABLE FROM

GMC Publications

BOOKS

MAGAZINES

EXOTIC GARDENING ◆ WATER GARDENING ◆ GARDEN CALENDAR
OUTDOOR PHOTOGRAPHY ◆ THE DOLL'S HOUSE MAGAZINE ◆ WOODTURNING
WOODCARVING ◆ WOODWORKING ◆ FURNITURE & CABINETMAKING
THE ROUTER ◆ BUSINESSMATTERS

The above represents a selection of titles available direct from the Publishers or through bookshops, newsagents and specialist retailers. To place an order, or to obtain a complete catalogue, contact:

GMC Publications,
Castle Place, 166 High Street, Lewes, East Sussex BN7 1XU, United Kingdom
Tel: 01273 488005 Fax: 01273 478606 Email: pubs@thegmcgroup.com
Orders by credit card are accepted